THE CONSOLATION
OF PHILOSOPHY

Mich / Andy

The Library of Liberal Arts
OSKAR PIEST, FOUNDER

THE CONSOLATION
OF PHILOSOPHY

BOETHIUS

Translated, with introduction and notes, by
RICHARD GREEN

. . . .

The Library of Liberal Arts

published by
Macmillan Publishing Company
New York
Collier Macmillan Publishers
London

Anicius Manlius Severinus Boethius: c. A.D. 480-524

Macmillan Publishing Company
866 Third Avenue
New York, New York, 10022
Collier Macmillan Canada, Inc.

First Edition
PRINTING   28   YEAR   0 1 2 3 4 5

Library of Congress Catalog Card Number 62-11788
ISBN: 0-02-346450-X

PREFACE

This translation is based on the critical edition of *The Consolation of Philosophy* by William Weinberger in the Corpus Scriptorum Ecclesiasticorum Latinorum (Vienna, 1934). I have checked my translation against the now standard critical edition by Ludwig Bieler, *Boethii Philosophiae Consolatio* (Turnhout, 1957). I have also used the excellent and convenient edition and translation prepared for The Loeb Classical Library by E. K. Rand and H. F. Stewart (Cambridge, Mass., 1918), both for comparing the Latin texts and as a check on my own readings of ambiguous passages. My purpose in this translation has been to provide students and the general reader with an accurate version of this famous medieval book in modern, idiomatic English.

The translator of *The Consolation* faces a number of serious problems. Boethius is one of the makers of the vocabulary of medieval philosophy, and employs many technical terms for which the English of the twentieth century provides no corresponding terms or, at best, terms which miss or confuse the precise meanings and distinctions of the medieval author. In many instances, Boethius' context makes the meaning of his philosophical terminology reasonably clear. Where it does not, I have tried to represent his ideas as nearly as I could in the language at my disposal.

The metrical parts of *The Consolation* raise further problems. Translators who have rendered these in verse have inevitably been forced by the demands of their art rather far from the meaning of the original. Since fidelity to the author's ideas, rather than imitation of his forms, has been my primary concern, I have chosen to translate his poems in prose and as literally as I could. In addition, this decision was influenced by my concern to preserve for the student of late medieval literature the figures and metaphors of this very influential

v

book. I hope that what is gained in fidelity to the historical language of the metrical passages will compensate for the loss of poetic reach and elegance which a good verse translation can provide.

Boethius was a devoted and learned reader of the ancient Latin authors and an expert medieval imitator of the prose style of Cicero, the Roman whom he most admired. As a consequence, his own prose is consciously mannered in ways which resist literal translation into modern English. I have not hesitated to alter the structure of his sentences where this could be done without changing his meaning.

Like all modern students of *The Consolation of Philosophy*, I am indebted to the work of E. K. Rand, Howard R. Patch, Helen M. Barrett, Edmund T. Silk, and Pierre Courcelle, and would like here to acknowledge generally points which might have been noted specifically in my Introduction and translation. In addition, I wish to thank my friends, Professors Alba H. Warren, Jr. and D. W. Robertson, Jr., for their careful reading of the translation, and for suggestions which have made it more accurate and graceful than it would otherwise have been.

RICHARD H. GREEN

Baltimore, Maryland
April, 1962

CONTENTS

INTRODUCTION

The Consolation of Philosophy was one of the most popular and influential books in Western Europe from the time it was written, in 524, until the end of the Renaissance. Its doctrine was a cornerstone of medieval humanism, its style a model of much important philosophical poetry in the late Middle Ages. The subject of the work is human happiness and the possibility of achieving it in the midst of the suffering and disappointment which play so large a part in every man's experience. *The Consolation* can still be read with interest in the twentieth century, not only because it is a landmark in the history of Western thought, but because its subject is of no less concern now than it was then. And, since the problem and its solution are presented poetically as well as doctrinally, succeeding ages have found in Boethius' work a remedy against desolation of the spirit which has never lost its curative power.

Like all great works, this one was made for more than its own time. Boethius wrote his book in prison after he had personally tested the power of wisdom to free the mind from the bondage imposed by its own failures as well as by forces of evil outside itself. He spoke to a world which believed in God as the creator and governor of man and the universe, and which regarded man's life on earth as a troubled exile in an alien land full of false and dangerous diversions from the true path of the soul's journey toward an eternal life of beatitude. For the reader of the Christian Middle Ages, *The Consolation of Philosophy* celebrated the life of the mind, or reason, and the possibility of its ultimate victory over the misfortunes and frustrations which attend fallen man's pursuit of transitory substitutes for the Supreme Good which alone can satisfy human desires.

The Consolation is a popularization, in the best sense, of

ix

philosophical and theological ideas; like the popular work of some philosophers and theologians in our own time, it was written not only for professionals but for the general reader. The book remains an important text in the history of philosophical speculation, and was appealed to as an authority by professional philosophers and theologians in later centuries; but its general popularity and its pervasive influence in later literature derive from its humane consideration of profound human problems which have confronted all men everywhere. The apparent power and success of injustice, fraud, and senseless cruelty against the apparent weakness and failure of reason and virtue is a dismaying part of the common experience of mankind. Attempts to account for the disparity between man's godlike aspirations and animal failures, to discover the grounds for distinguishing between good and evil human action, to evaluate the relative importance of the things men strive for, belong to man's earliest and latest efforts to know himself and to assess the value of his experience. Boethius' work was at once a synthesis of the best that had been achieved before his time, and a new formulation of the solution which was to be part of the philosophical basis of Christian ethics for over a thousand years.

THE AUTHOR

The deep personal involvement of the author in the problems of which he writes, as well as the weight of his authority in other areas of medieval learning, suggest the importance of a brief account of his life and of the circumstances in which *The Consolation of Philosophy* was composed. Boethius was born about 480 into the distinguished Roman family of the Anicii. After the death of his father, who had been Consul in 487, the boy was adopted by the even more distinguished Symmachus, and later married his guardian's daughter Rusticiana. He received the best education to be had in those troubled times, and his mastery of the full range of late classical and early medieval learning is shown by the variety and authority of his published work.

Early in his career Boethius learned Greek and undertook to translate and comment on all the works of Aristotle and Plato with the intention of demonstrating their essential agreement. Although the press of public business and his early death made it impossible for him to pursue this ambitious program very far, the variety and excellence of his achievement made him a figure of major importance in the world of learning for over a thousand years. To provide an introduction to the study of logic he translated and commented on Porphyry's *Introduction to the Categories of Aristotle,* a book designed to introduce students to problems of dialectical and epistemological method; it was this commentary which provided the point of departure for the controversy between realists and nominalists on the existence of universals, which was to be so important in later medieval philosophy. He also translated the four logical works which make up Aristotle's *Organon,* and wrote commentaries on two of them. In addition, he wrote a commentary on Cicero's *Topics,* and five essays of his own on logic. It is not too much to say that the study of logic in the Middle Ages, and therefore an essential part of its modes of inquiry and discourse, were founded on the work of Boethius both in his transmission of the texts of classical dialectics and in the direction provided by his commentaries.

In addition to these works devoted to the third of the disciplines of the medieval trivium, Boethius wrote works on arithmetic, geometry, music, and probably one on astronomy, some of which were to become standard texts in the medieval schools. Finally, he extended the range of his intellectual interests to the summit of medieval learning in at least four treatises on various problems of theology. When we add to this impressive record the status of *The Consolation of Philosophy* in the medieval study of moral philosophy, we begin to see the full dimensions of Boethius' fame and authority.

But Boethius was a man of public affairs as well as a scholar. While still a young man he was led by the responsibilities of his position as a member of an aristocratic senatorial family, and by the distinguished examples of his father and guardian, to enter the Roman administrative system. As a philosopher, he felt keenly the force of Plato's teaching that the government of the commonwealth ought to be in the hands of wise men, and that those who were appointed to rule ought to be philosophers. He became Consul in 510, when he was about thirty, and thereafter was closely identified with the interests of the Senate. At the time of his political downfall, in 523, he was Master of the King's Offices, one of the highest positions in the Western Empire. In addition to his personal successes in the public service, he had seen his sons follow in his footsteps to become joint Consuls in 522.

The events which brought about the ruin of this extraordinary scholar and statesman are of special interest, since they are the immediate occasion of *The Consolation*. In 523, when Boethius was in his early forties and at the peak of his fortune and power, he suffered a sudden reversal of fortune which led to disgrace, exile, and finally to execution. In his own account of his troubles, Boethius lists four charges brought against him: that he desired the safety of the Senate; that he hindered the use of perjured testimony against the Senate; that he desired the freedom of Rome; that he was guilty of sacrilege by magical contact with evil spirits. The political nature of the charges against him is supported by the contemporary historical record, and the situation in the Empire at the time was one in which the Roman patriot was unusually vulnerable.

Theodoric, King of the Ostrogoths, had invaded Italy in 489 and had consolidated his power legally in 493 by becoming Roman Governor technically subject to the Emperor in the East. He had preserved the Senate and the consular administrative system, though he kept effective power in his own capable and autocratic hands. Theodoric seems to have been an efficient and just ruler, and under his reign the Empire in the West prospered. He was an Arian Christian, and therefore a heretic in the eyes of his Roman subjects; [1] but in this area too, he acted with temperate justice and tolerance. How was it, then, that a ruler with a reputation for fair dealing ordered the imprisonment and execution of a high official in his administration whose intelligence and virtue seemed everywhere acknowledged? The answer appears to lie in the nature of the alleged crimes; for the charge of treason is one to which men of independent judgment and deeply held principles are always vulnerable in an autocratic government. Even under the absolute rule of the Gothic King, the Roman Senate was jealous of its historic prerogatives; and Boethius stresses his concern for the Senate. Such devotion to an assembly which was conscious of its former greatness might easily be construed as disloyalty to an alien ruler, especially if, as Boethius says, and contemporary historians confirm, he was the victim of perjured testimony and forged letters. Moreover, it is probable, as William Bark [2] has shown, that Boethius was involved in the efforts to reestablish doctrinal and ecclesiastical unity between Rome and the Empire in the East. At a time when theological and political matters were closely connected, Boethius' involvement might easily have been construed as treasonable by the Arian Theodoric. The King may have been misinformed by political enemies of the Magister Officiorum, or he may have regarded Boethius and Symmachus, who was also executed, as conspirators in an

---

[1] The Arian Christians, followers of the doctrinal position of Arius (d. A.D. 336), held that Christ was neither truly God nor truly man: he did not exist coeternally with God but was a created being, therefore was only semidivine; and, though he took a human body through which he acted, he had divine essence rather than a human soul, therefore was not truly man. Thus they departed from the Catholic position of Christ as true God and true man, as pronounced at the Council of Nicaea in A.D. 325. Theodoric's subjects were chiefly Catholics, as was Justin, the Emperor of the East.

[2] "Theodoric vs. Boethius: Vindication and Apology," *American Historical Review*, XLIX (1944), 410-26; and see also Bark's *Origins of the Medieval World* (New York, 1960).

attempt to reunite East and West politically as well as doctrinally.

The final charge of sacrilege, the invocation of evil spirits, is another to which men devoted to the life of the intellect are peculiarly vulnerable because it can be used to change popular acclaim to suspicion and condemnation. Boethius was a mathematician and astronomer, as well as a philosopher, at a time when these studies were easily associated in the public imagination with magic and the probing of forbidden mysteries. Boethius himself is most dismayed by the realization that his devotion to philosophy was itself enough to make him the object of popular suspicion. He sees in his personal ruin the weakening of general public virtue and the encouragement of forces in society which greed and ignorance will drive to any excess.

As a result of these charges, Boethius was condemned by the very Senate he had tried to defend, was stripped of his honor and possessions, and thrown into a remote prison where he was ultimately executed. Such were the misfortunes which forced this philosopher-statesman to re-examine the principles upon which his life was based. *The Consolation of Philosophy* is his record of the victory of reason and hope over the despair brought on by personal disaster. Boethius chose to incorporate his own record of these events into the autobiographical part of *The Consolation,* to involve himself and his personal experience in the representation of the recovery of certain moral truths, and their implications, which he held to be valid for all men.

THE POET AS PHILOSOPHER

The Consolation of Philosophy is a work of moral philosophy directing men toward the discovery and enjoyment of the supreme good, the object of desire capable of fulfilling perfectly the best of human aspirations. The author begins with a dramatic description of the desperate consequences of misfortune and finds their cause in man's pursuit of various kinds of transitory and limited goals which seem to promise happiness. Riches, honors, power, fame and pleasure are brought under the philosopher's scrutiny; they are found to be legitimate but partial objects of desire, useful as means toward the attainment of the perfect good, but inadequate and disappointing as ends in themselves. Those who set their hearts on any or all of these limited means of happiness are doomed to disappointment, for the possession of them cannot fully satisfy and, worst of all, they may be lost either accidentally or through the vicious actions of others. Only God, the supreme good and source of perfect happiness, can fully satisfy the desires of man's rational nature; and the happiness which love of God affords cannot be taken away through misfortune, for it is within man and wholly dependent on his own rational control. The liberating power of the mind, the self-mastery which comes from a just estimate of the limited value of material, and therefore transitory, satisfactions, is the basis of Boethius' ethical doctrine.

The assumptions upon which Boethius' philosophical position rests, and the detailed arguments by which his position is expressed are, for the most part, not original. By the time *The Consolation* was written they were the common possession of educated men, derived from the classic works of Greek and Roman philosophy, most notably from Plato, Aristotle, and Cicero, and from the Neoplatonists, and adapted during the patristic period to the theology of Christian revelation. What is new in *The Consolation,* and the reason for its lasting influence and importance in the history of medieval philosophy, is the expert synthesis of these traditional ethical doctrines by an author who consciously limits his consideration to the powers of natural reason without direct recourse, or even mention of, Christian revelation. Nothing in *The Consolation* is inconsistent with patristic theology; indeed, precedent for nearly every idea which Boethius proposes can be found in the work of St. Augustine. For Augustine, too, had honored the "Platonists," and had drawn much from their teaching about the supreme good which, when it is possessed, satisfies all human needs and wishes. Augustine observed that Plato had identified this highest good with God, and therefore adopted Plato's definition of the philosopher as one who loves God and directs his pursuit of wisdom toward the enjoyment of that blessedness which comes from the possession of the supreme good.

The effects of the hundred years which separate these early Christian writers can be observed in their attitudes toward classical philosophy. For Augustine, the late Roman version of Platonism was still a powerful antagonist which drove him to polemical criticism of those aspects which he found incompatible with Biblical revelation, and to a rather cautious praise of those doctrines which he found appropriate and useful. He was primarily a theologian devoted to the formation of Christian doctrine, and moral philosophy was only a part of his enterprise. Historical circumstances made the success of his undertaking almost immediate, so that a hundred years later Boethius could write as a Christian philosopher and classical scholar without apology or polemic, defining and limiting the scope of his attention and the mode of his discourse to human nature and the natural possibilities of human wisdom.

Boethius' relations to earlier classical and Christian thought may be illustrated in his handling of the issue of temporal fortune and misfortune. The conception of Fortune as the feminine personification of changeable, unpredictable fate is drawn from pagan sources, notably from the Roman poets and moralists, where she is described as blind, vagrant, inconstant, meretricious. But, as Seneca had observed, there are limits to her power: she cannot give a man virtue, nor deprive him of it, and so virtue becomes the wise man's weapon against her. She represented fate as a random, uncontrollable force, to be feared or courted, opposed or despised, according to the theological and philosophical dispositions of those who, largely through the experience of misfortune, felt her power. From the Stoic notion that fortune could be opposed, or rather, successfully endured, by the exercise of reason and the practice of virtue, the early Christian theologians developed a doctrine which made Fortune a figure of fate, and fate a part of the divine government of the world, thus effectively depriving both fortune and fate of any real existence as independent and potentially destructive forces. Augustine observed that temporal prosperity and adversity are not signs of demonic intervention in the lives of men, nor of the favor or disfavor of the true God; they are simply decreed and permitted by the One whose wisdom is perfect, and who can will only good for men, but whose judgments cannot be fully comprehended and therefore should not be complained of. He scoffs at the pagan worship of a blind goddess dispensing adversity and prosperity at random; but he applauds those pagan philosophers who understood fate to be that series of ordered causes which carry out the disposition of the divine will, and he quotes with approval the doctrine of Seneca that fate is the manifestation of divine power irresistibly worked out in temporal events. Even the actions of wicked men, which are contrary to God's will, are, through the inscrutable divine wisdom and power, made to serve "those just and good ends and outcomes which He Himself has foreknown." [3]

A century later, Boethius transformed the pagan goddess into a fictional figure embodying man's limited hopes of temporal prosperity and his fears of adversity. Fortune is a way, and the wrong way, of regarding fate; and all men are subject to her in the sense that uncertainty and change, pleasure, anxiety, and depression are the ordinary lot of man. But, if subjection to fortune is a fact of experience, it is nevertheless possible for the man of reason to bear misfortune with equanimity of spirit, even to rise above fortune to the enjoyment of profound happiness based on a wise appraisal of the true values of things which men naturally desire. For the wise man, fortune is a specious identification of fate; the course of events which affect his life may seem random and capricious, and most of them are indeed beyond his control;

[3] St. Augustine, *De civitate Dei* XXII. 2.

but if his intelligence leads him to acknowledge the existence of a divine power which governs the universe and every individual man, and if the Creator is the perfect Good who wills only good, then whatever the Good does or permits must be good, however painful and unjust the temporal consequences may seem to be.

Boethius undertook to justify the ways of God to men, to explore philosophically the mysteries of the divine will as it is manifested in the order, and apparent disorder, of temporal events. Drawing upon his extensive reading of the Greek and Roman writers, he attempts a rational reconciliation of man's feeling that he is victimized by forces beyond his control with his belief in a divine Governor of the universe. To the pursuit of unstable temporal prosperity, with its uncertain and short-lived felicities, Boethius opposes the idea that for rational natures true happiness is to be found only in the enjoyment of One who transcends the flux of the material and temporal. The perfection which belongs to the divine nature, its simplicity, truth, and goodness, constitutes at once the model and goal of human nature, the only adequate object of human imitation and desire. And since the world of natural and human events must be subject to God's providential government (for to argue otherwise would imply some lack in the divine power), the wise man must grant that whatever is, and whatever happens, must ultimately be according to God's providential will.

Boethius was keenly aware that his doctrine raises the problem of the freedom of man's will. For if God knows everything, and if his knowledge determines whatever will happen, how can men choose freely to do one thing rather than another. The Boethian answer, given in Book Five of *The Consolation*, again parallels the Augustinian, and both Christian authors turn their arguments on the position taken by Cicero in his *De divinatione*. In Augustine's reading, Cicero denies divine foreknowledge in the process of denying fatal determination in order to preserve human free will and responsibility as the basis of social order. Augustine's solution is to affirm both divine prescience and human freedom, "for our wills themselves are included in the order of causes which is known by God, and so are a part of his foreknowledge, inasmuch as human wills are themselves causes of human actions; and He who foreknew all the causes of things would certainly know our wills among those causes." [4] The logical difficulty is simply resolved by affirming that both sides of an apparent contradiction must be true: God must know all things, otherwise He would not be God; and man must be able to choose freely because his experience tells him that he can and does, and because free choice is a part of man's obligation to live well. Such direct confrontation of problem and experience was possible for the theologian, but it was not possible for the logician. As a Christian, Boethius had to arrive at Augustine's affirmation of divine omniscience and human freedom; as a logician and speculative philosopher he formulated a solution, based on the difference between human and divine knowledge, which was to be authoritative for centuries to come.

THE PHILOSOPHER AS POET

Such, in brief, is the philosophical substance of *The Consolation;* but these largely traditional ideas do not explain the enduring fame of Boethius' book among educated readers, nor its extraordinary influence on the poets of later ages. *The Consolation of Philosophy* is more than a synthesis of early medieval moral philosophy; it is an original work of imaginative art. The philosopher-statesman had personally endured the full measure of misfortune and near despair of which he writes. He had tested the value of his philosophy in recovering a clear view of the sources and aims of such happiness as men can reasonably achieve. In this victory of rational aspiration over misdirected desire he had found the serene self-possession which made his book possible; and, since he was a

---

[4] *De civitate Dei* V. 9; cf. Cicero, *De divinatione* II. 8.

poet as well as a philosopher, Boethius was able to represent his experience in a fictional vision over which he exercised a deliberate artistic control.

The Consolation is, in its form, a philosophical dialogue after the manner of Plato and Cicero. It is also a satura, a medley of prose and verse parts, and the verse sections themselves are a medley of classical forms. Boethius found his immediate model in The Marriage of Mercury and Philology by Martianus Capella; a hundred years before Boethius composed his work, Martianus had exploited the obvious possibilities of the Menippean satire [5] for the purpose of an attractive and persuasive presentation of philosophical ideas. Both works became standard texts in the curriculum of the medieval schools, and models for other exercises in the same form. In The Consolation, Boethius ostensibly uses the poems for purposes of rest and refreshment: Philosophy remarks in the opening section of Book Two that she intends to cure the sickness of her patient gradually, and that she will use the sweet persuasion of rhetoric and the grace of music to prepare him for the strong medicine of the highest philosophical speculation. Later, in the third prose of the same book, the narrator acknowledges that he has found the rhetoric and poetry persuasive, but finds the relief only temporary. In Book Four, when Philosophy becomes engrossed in her explanation of the crucial relations between Providence and Fate, she says that the narrator will have to forego the pleasures of verse until she finishes her argument. The reiteration of this attitude may suggest that Boethius is here reflecting the medieval estimate of poetry as one of the lower arts ancillary to the more serious pursuit of dialectic in the hierarchy of learning. This same attitude is evident in the violence of Philosophy's condemnation of the Muses of poetry as wholly inadequate to rescue the dreamer from his despair. On the other hand, it is equally clear that Boethius had a much higher estimate

[5] The term derives from Menippus, a Greek cynic and satirist of the third century B.C. whose works, none of which are extant, were written in a mixture of prose and verse.

of the value of poetry than this seems to imply. In addition
to a familiarity with ancient poetry which made apt quotation and allusion from memory possible to him in prison, he
chose to make *The Consolation* a poetic vision and included
in it some excellent poems. It is true that some of the metrical
pieces offer little more than brief general comment on the
preceding prose argument, or classical examples of the moral
situations which Philosophy describes; but others are profound syntheses of the philosophical implications of the
argument, reaching beyond Philosophy's dialectic to an in-
tuitive grasp of the mysterious truth toward which the rational argument is directed. Such, for example, is the dreamer's prayer in Book One, Poem Five, in which Boethius
concludes the autobiographical account of his disastrous misfortunes with an appeal to the Creator of the star-filled universe to govern the destinies of men with that perfect harmony which rules the rest of nature. And, at the conclusion
of Book Two, Philosophy returns to the same theme to sing
of that divine love which is the governing principle of cosmic
harmony and therefore ought to govern the souls of men and
women. Perhaps the greatest poem in *The Consolation* appears at the momentous point in Book Three (Poem Nine)
when Philosophy implores divine help before she begins to
show that God, the Supreme Good, and perfect happiness are
one and the same. In twenty-eight lines of astonishing poetic
concentration and power, Boethius explores the central theological and cosmological ideas of Plato's *Timaeus* and fits
them to his own conception of a personal God and to the
whole process of his poetic vision.

The poetic quality of *The Consolation* which most influenced later medieval poetry, however, was not the skillful
handling of the *prosimetrum* form, nor the excellence of the
individual poems, but the author's use of the fictional vision
as a frame for philosophical speculation and moral persuasion. Throughout the Middle Ages, poetry was made to please
and to teach, or, more precisely, to please *in order* to teach.
The truth of the poet's experience was his primary concern;

his mode of representation was chosen for its appropriateness and rhetorical effectiveness. The possibilities of the dream-vision as a poetic mode for the presentation of philosophical ideas had been treated by Macrobius late in the fourth century in his *Commentary on Cicero's Dream of Scipio,* a work of primary authority and pervasive influence during the whole Middle Ages. In the early pages of his *Commentary,* Macrobius justifies the use of fictional visions by the philosopher-poet as a means of presenting natural and divine truths for the promotion of virtuous human behavior. The veil of fiction in *The Consolation of Philosophy* is nearly transparent: the narrator of the vision is quickly identified, partly as the author who had indeed achieved the consolation which philosophy could provide, partly as every man who finds himself in similar circumstances and is willing to undergo the salutary experience represented by the poet's fiction. The figure of Lady Philosophy is recognized at once, by name and description, as the highest natural wisdom which man can aspire to; and her rival, Fortune, is immediately recognized as the personification of temporal prosperity and adversity which can dominate and enslave her unwary victims.

A history of the continuing influence of Boethius' fictional mode in later medieval poetry would include Alan of Lille's Dreamer, in *The Complaint of Nature,* who is instructed by Lady Nature to avoid the snares of her rival, the monstrous Venus; the feminine figure of Reason, in the *Roman de la Rose,* who contends unsuccessfully for the service of the dreaming Lover in competition with Venus and her son, the God of Love. Dante's Lady "Philosophy" in his *Convivio* and even Beatrice, in a much more complicated way, in his *Commedia,* are partly derived from Boethius' Philosophy. The feminine figures in Chaucer's vision poems, most obviously Nature and Lady Fame, are her literary descendants; and so are the two ladies in the first of Will's visions in *Piers Plowman,* Holy Church and Lady Meed. The persons in the vision poetry of the later Middle Ages were, for the most part, more realistically drawn than their antecedents in *The Consolation,* and the circumstances of the visionary encounters with them were more elaborately and imaginatively portrayed. Nevertheless, they continued to represent philosophical ideas and moral attitudes moving freely, unbound by realistic demands of space and time, in the realm of poetic imagination.

Finally, Boethius' expert use of traditional metaphors in his description of every man's confrontation of the forces of good and evil both enhanced the poetic quality of his own work and supported the life of these basic images in the work of later poets. The author's own literal imprisonment becomes a figure of the soul's imprisonment in the body, the bondage imposed by the demands of the passions, the enslavement to Fortune and her deceitful favors. His exile from Rome represents his separation from the true country of the mind, a self-imposed wandering in an alien land of transitory satisfactions which make him forget what is truly good and the source of genuine human happiness. The condition of Fortune's victim is described as a sickness, a disease of the mind leading to anxiety, lethargy, and despair. Philosophy is the physician whose medicines of rational, and therefore human, judgment can restore his soul to health. The condition of man enslaved by devotion to Fortune is described as blindness; the light of the mind has gone out, leaving the sufferer oppressed by the dark clouds of mortal desires. Philosophy is an embodied splendor whose presence can dispel the dark night of despair and by reflecting the light of truth can bring her students to the dawn of recognition, the remembrance of the sun of divine truth. If these metaphors strike us as somewhat old fashioned, we might bear in mind not so much that these modes of expression were newer then, for they were quite conventional in the early sixth century, but that Boethius was writing for readers who valued the traditional as authoritative, and who therefore set far less store in the novel and idiosyncratic than we do.

RICHARD H. GREEN

SELECTED BIBLIOGRAPHY

Bark, William. "The Legend of Boethius' Martyrdom," *Speculum*, XXI (1946), 312-17.

Barrett, H. M. *Boethius: Some Aspects of His Time and Work.* Cambridge, 1940.

Bieler, Ludovicus. *Boethii Philosophiae Consolatio.* "Corpus Christianorum," ser. lat., XCIV. Turnhout, 1957.

Courcelle, P. *Les lettres grecques en occident de Macrobe à Cassiodore.* 2nd edn. Paris, 1948.

Patch, H. R. *The Tradition of Boethius: A Study of his Importance in Mediaeval Culture.* New York, 1935.

Rand, E. K. *Founders of the Middle Ages.* Cambridge, Mass., 1929.

Silk, E. T. "Boethius's *Consolation of Philosophy* as a Sequel to Augustine's Dialogues and Soliloquies," *Harvard Theological Review*, XXXII (1939), 19-39.

Stewart, H. F., and E. K. Rand. *Boethius: The Theological Tractates and The Consolation of Philosophy.* "The Loeb Classical Library." Cambridge, Mass. and London, 1918.

Weinberger, Wilhelm. *Boethii Philosophiae Consolationis Libri Quinque.* "Corpus Scriptorum Ecclesiasticorum Latinorum," LXVII. Leipzig, 1934.

NOTE ON THE TEXT

For a discussion of the text on which this translation is based, and of the translation of the alternating prose-poem sections in the original text, the reader is invited to see the translator's Preface. Within the framework of Boethius' narration, Professor Green has added quotation marks to the dialogue between Lady Philosophy and Boethius, thus identifying the speakers. He has also provided annotation explaining and identifying allusions and references, explanatory headings to the prose sections, and a short summary of each of the five Books.

The Editors

THE CONSOLATION OF PHILOSOPHY

BOOK I

Poem 1

I who once wrote songs with keen delight am now by sorrow driven to take up melancholy measures. Wounded Muses tell me what I must write, and elegiac verses bathe my face with real tears. Not even terror could drive from me these faithful companions of my long journey. Poetry, which was once the glory of my happy and flourishing youth, is still my comfort in this misery of my old age.

Old age has come too soon with its evils, and sorrow has commanded me to enter the age which is hers. My hair is prematurely gray, and slack skin shakes on my exhausted body. Death, happy to men when she does not intrude in the sweet years, but comes when often called in sorrow, turns a deaf ear to the wretched and cruelly refuses to close weeping eyes.

The sad hour that has nearly drowned me came just at the time that faithless Fortune favored me with her worthless gifts. Now that she has clouded her deceitful face, my accursed life seems to go on endlessly. My friends, why did you so often think me happy? Any man who has fallen never stood securely.

Prose 1

Lady Philosophy appears to him and drives away the Muses of poetry.

While I silently pondered these things, and decided to write down my wretched complaint, there appeared standing above me a woman of majestic countenance whose flashing eyes seemed wise beyond the ordinary wisdom of men. Her color was bright, suggesting boundless vigor, and yet she seemed so old that she could not be thought of as belonging to our age. Her height seemed to vary: sometimes she seemed of ordinary human stature, then again her head seemed to touch the top of the heavens. And when she raised herself to her full height she penetrated heaven itself, beyond the vision of human eyes. Her clothing was made of the most delicate threads, and by the most exquisite workmanship; it had—as she afterwards told me—been woven by her own hands into an everlasting fabric. Her clothes had been darkened in color somewhat by neglect and the passage of time, as happens to pictures exposed to smoke. At the lower edge of her robe was woven a Greek Π, at the top the letter Θ, and between them were seen clearly marked stages, like stairs, ascending from the lowest level to the highest.[1] This robe had been torn, however, by the hands of violent men, who had ripped away what they could. In her right hand, the woman held certain books; in her left hand, a scepter.

When she saw the Muses of poetry standing beside my bed and consoling me with their words, she was momentarily upset and glared at them with burning eyes.[2] "Who let these whores from the theater come to the bedside of this sick man?" she said. "They cannot offer medicine for his sorrows; they will nourish him only with their sweet poison. They kill the fruitful harvest of reason with the sterile thorns of the passions; they do not liberate the minds of men from disease, but

[1] Π and Θ are the first letters of the Greek words for the two divisions of philosophy, theoretical and practical. Boethius wrote (*In Porph. Dial.* I. 3): ". . . for philosophy is a genus of which there are two species, one of which is called theoretical, the other practical, that is, speculative and active."

[2] Boethius' condemnation of the Muses provided the enemies of poetry in the later Middle Ages with a powerful, if specious, argument. In his authoritative and influential *Genealogy of the Gods*, Boccaccio argues that Boethius is here condemning only a certain kind of obscene theatrical poetry; he cites Boethius' extensive use of ancient poetry and myth as evidence of a high regard for poetry. See *Boccaccio on Poetry*, tr. C. G. Osgood, "Library of Liberal Arts," No. 82 (New York, 1956), pp. 94-96.

merely accustom them to it. I would find it easier to bear if
your flattery had, as it usually does, seduced some ordinary
dull-witted man; in that case, it would have been no concern
of mine. But this man has been educated in the philosophical
schools of the Eleatics and the Academy.[3] Get out, you Sirens;
your sweetness leads to death. Leave him to be cured and
made strong by my Muses."

And so the defeated Muses, shamefaced and with downcast
eyes, went sadly away. My sight was so dimmed by tears that
I could not tell who this woman of imperious authority might
be, and I lay there astonished, my eyes staring at the earth,
silently waiting to see what she would do. She came nearer
and sat at the foot of my bed. When she noticed my grief-
stricken, downcast face, she reproved my anxiety with this
song.

POEM 2

"Alas! how this mind is dulled, drowned in the over-
whelming depths. It wanders in outer darkness, deprived of
its natural light. Sick anxiety, inflated by worldly winds,
swells his thoughts to bursting.

"Once this man was free beneath the open heaven, and
he used to run along heavenly paths. He saw the splendor
of the red sun, the heaven of the cold moon. And any star
that pursued its vagrant paths, returning through various
spheres, this master understood by his computations.

"Beyond all this, he sought the causes of things: why the
sighing winds vex the seawaves; what spirit turns the stable
world; and why the sun rises out of the red east to fall beneath the western ocean. He sought to know what tempers
the gentle hours of spring and makes them adorn the earth

---

3 The Eleatics represent a school of Greek philosophy at Elia in Italy.
Zeno, one of its members in the fifth century B.C., was thought to be the
inventor of dialectic, the art of reasoning about matters of opinion. The
Academy is the traditional name for Plato's school of philosophy.

with rosy flowers; what causes fertile autumn to flow with bursting grapes in a good year.

"This man used to explore and reveal Nature's secret causes. Now he lies here, bound down by heavy chains, the light of his mind gone out; his head is bowed down and he is forced to stare at the dull earth.

PROSE 2

Seeing his desperate condition, Philosophy speaks more gently and promises to cure him.

"But," she said, "it is time for medicine rather than complaint." Fixing me with her eyes, she said: "Are you not he who once was nourished by my milk and brought up on my food; who emerged from weakness to the strength of a virile soul? I gave you weapons that would have protected you with invincible power, if you had not thrown them away. Don't you recognize me? Why don't you speak? Is it shame or astonishment that makes you silent? I'd rather it were shame, but I see that you are overcome by shock." When she saw that I was not only silent but struck dumb, she gently laid her hand on my breast and said: "There is no danger. You are suffering merely from lethargy, the common illness of deceived minds. You have forgotten yourself a little, but you will quickly be yourself again when you recognize me. To bring you to your senses, I shall quickly wipe the dark cloud of mortal things from your eyes." Then, she dried my tear-filled eyes with a fold of her robe.

POEM 3

Then, when the night was over, darkness left me and my eyes regained their former strength; just as when the stars are covered by swift Corus, and the sky is darkened by storm clouds, the sun hides and the stars do not shine;

night comes down to envelop the earth. But if Boreas, blowing from his Thracian cave, beats and lays open the hiding day, then Phoebus shines forth, glittering with sudden light, and strikes our astonished eyes with his rays.[4]

PROSE 3

Boethius recognizes Lady Philosophy. She promises to help him as she has always helped those who love and serve her.

In a similar way, I too was able to see the heavens again when the clouds of my sorrow were swept away; I recovered my judgment and recognized the face of my physician. When I looked at her closely, I saw that she was Philosophy, my nurse, in whose house I had lived from my youth. "Mistress of all virtues," I said, "why have you come, leaving the arc of heaven, to this lonely desert of our exile? Are you a prisoner, too, charged as I am with false accusations?"

She answered, "How could I desert my child, and not share with you the burden of sorrow you carry, a burden caused by hatred of my name? Philosophy has never thought it right to leave the innocent man alone on his journey. Should I fear to face my accusers, as though their enmity were something new? Do you suppose that this is the first time wisdom has been attacked and endangered by wicked men? We fought against such rashness and folly long ago, even before the time of our disciple Plato. And in Plato's own time, his master Socrates, with my help, merited the victory of an unjust death.[5] Afterwards, the inept schools of Epicureans, Stoics, and others, each seeking its own interests, tried to steal the inheritance of Socrates and to possess me (in spite of my protests and strug-

---

4 Corus, the north-west wind; Boreas, the north wind. Thrace, part of modern Turkey, was regarded by the ancients as an extreme northern place. Phoebus is the sun.

5 Socrates was accused of corrupting youth and ridiculing the gods. In 399 B.C., the Athenian state condemned him to death (by drinking poison). For a description of the death scene of Socrates, see Plato, *Phaedo* 115a-118.

gles), as though I were the spoils of their quarreling. They tore this robe which I had woven with my own hands and, having ripped off some little pieces of it, went away supposing that they possessed me wholly.[6] Then, when traces of my garments were seen on some of them, they were rashly thought to be my friends, and they were therefore condemned by the error of the profane mob.

"Perhaps you have not heard of the banishment of Anaxagoras, the poisoning of Socrates, the torments of Zeno,[7] for these men were strange to you. But you probably know about Canius, Seneca, and Soranus,[8] for their fame is recent and widely known. They were disgraced only because they had been trained in my studies and therefore seemed obnoxious to wicked men. You should not be surprised, then, if we are blown about by stormy winds in the voyage of this life, since our main duty is to oppose the wicked. But, even though our enemies are numerous, we should spurn them because they are without leadership and are driven frantically this way and that by error. And if they sometimes attack us with extraordinary force, our leader withdraws her followers into a fortress,

[6] Boethius, and most other medieval thinkers until the late thirteenth century, regarded Plato as the greatest of the ancient philosophers. Philosophy's robe is the figure of the unity of true philosophy; this unity was, in Boethius' opinion, shattered by such limited philosophies as Epicureanism, based on the principle of pleasure, and Stoicism, based on the principle that whatever happens must be accepted without grief or joy. Epicurus founded his school in Greece late in the fourth century B.C. The Stoic school was founded by Zeno of Athens at about the same time.

[7] Anaxagoras, a Greek astronomer and philosopher, was banished from Athens when his theory of the heavens led to his being accused of impiety. He was exiled about 450 B.C. Zeno of Elea (see p. 8) was tortured by Nearchus from whose tyranny he had sought to deliver his country. Boethius is comparing his own predicament to those of earlier philosophers who were punished for honoring their principles.

[8] Julius Canius was executed about A.D. 40 for reproaching the Roman Emperor Caligula. Seneca, the great Roman poet and philosopher of the first century, and a high public official under Nero, was accused of conspiracy by the emperor and forced to commit suicide. Soranus was also a victim of Nero's tyranny; he was condemned to death in A.D. 66.

leaving our enemies to waste their energies on worthless spoils. While they fight over things of no value, we laugh at them from above, safe from their fury and defended by a strength against which their aggressive folly cannot prevail.

POEM 4

"The serene man who has ordered his life stands above menacing fate and unflinchingly faces good and bad fortune. This virtuous man can hold up his head unconquered. The threatening and raging ocean storms which churn the waves cannot shake him; nor can the bursting furnace of Vesuvius, aimlessly throwing out its smoky fire; nor the fiery bolts of lightning which can topple the highest towers. Why then are we wretched, frightened by fierce tyrants who rage without the power to harm us? He who hopes for nothing and fears nothing can disarm the fury of these impotent men; but he who is burdened by fears and desires is not master of himself. He throws away his shield and retreats; he fastens the chain by which he will be drawn.

PROSE 4

Boethius gives an account of his public career and especially of the causes of his present misery.[9]

"Do you understand what I have told you," Philosophy asked; "have my words impressed you at all, or are you 'like the ass which cannot hear the lyre'?[10] Why are you crying? Speak out, don't hide what troubles you. If you want a doctor's help, you must uncover your wound."[11]

I pulled myself together and answered: "Do I have to ex-

[9] For a discussion of the historical circumstances of Boethius' imprisonment and death, see Introduction, pp. xii-xiv.

[10] Boethius here cites the Greek proverb: ὄνος λύρας.

[11] Cf. Homer, *Iliad* I. 363.

plain; isn't the misery of my misfortune evident enough? I should think this place alone would make you pity me. Compare this prison with my library at home which you chose as your own and in which you often discussed with me the knowledge of human and divine things. Did I look like this? Was I dressed this way when I studied nature's mysteries with you, when you mapped the courses of the stars for me with your geometer's rod, when you formed my moral standards and my whole view of life according to the norm of the heavenly order? [12] Are these miseries the rewards your servants should expect? You yourself proposed the course I have followed when you made Plato say that civil governments would be good if wise men were appointed rulers, or if those appointed to rule would study wisdom.[13] Further, you decreed in the words of the same philosopher that government of the commonwealth ought to be in the hands of wise men; that if it should be left to unscrupulous and wicked men, they would bring about the ruin of the good.[14]

"On this authority, I decided to apply to public administration the principles I had learned privately from you. You, and God who gave you to the minds of wise men, know that I became a magistrate only because of the unanimous wish of all good men. For these reasons I have become involved in grave and hopeless trouble with dishonest men; and, as always happens to the administrator of independent conscience, I have had to be willing to make powerful enemies in the interest of safeguarding justice.

"I have often opposed the greed of Conigastus in his swindling of the poor. I have condemned the crimes of Triguilla, Provost of the King's house, both in their beginnings and after they had been committed. At grave risk to my position I have protected the weak from the lies and avarice of cruel men in power. No man ever corrupted my administration of justice. I was as depressed as those who suffered the losses

[12] Cf. Plato, *Republic* 592b.
[13] Cf. Plato, *Republic* 473d, 487e.
[14] Cf. Plato, *Epistle X* 350b; *Republic* 347c.

when I saw the wealth of our citizens dissipated either by private fraud or oppressive taxation. At the time of the severe famine, when prices were set so exorbitantly high that the province of Campania seemed about to starve, I carried on the people's fight against the Praetorian Prefect himself and, with the King's approval, I won—the fixed prices were not enforced.

"I saved Paulinus, the former Consul, from the howling dogs of the court who hoped to devour his wealth. In order to save Albinus, another former Consul, from unjust punishment, I risked the hatred of his accuser, Cyprian. One would think I had stirred up enough opposition. But I ought to have been defended by others, especially since, through devotion to justice, I had given up the favor of the courtiers who might have saved me. But who were the accusers who overthrew me? One of them was Basil who had earlier been expelled from the King's service and was now forced by his debts to testify against me. My other accusers were Opilio and Gaudentius, also men banished by royal decree for their many corrupt practices. They tried to avoid exile by taking sanctuary, but when the King heard of it he decreed that, if they did not leave Ravenna by a certain day, they should be branded on the forehead and forcibly expelled. How could the King's judgment have been more severe? And yet on that very day their testimony against me was accepted. Why should this have happened? Did I deserve it? Did their criminal records make them just accusers? Fortune ought to have been shamed, if not by the innocence of the accused, then at least by the villainy of the accusers.

"Finally, what am I accused of? They say I desired the safety of the Senate. But how? I am convicted of having hindered their accuser from giving evidence that the Senate is guilty of treason. What is your judgment, my teacher? Shall I deny the charge in order to avoid shaming you? But I did desire to protect the Senate, and I always will. And how can I confess, since I have already stopped hindering their accuser? Shall I consider it a crime to have supported the integrity of

the Senate? It is true that the Senate itself, by its decrees
against me, has made my position a crime. But folly, driven
by self-deception, cannot change the merits of the case; nor,
following the rule of Socrates, can I think it right either to
hide the truth or concede a lie.[15] I leave it to you, and to
the judgment of the wise, whether my course of action is
right. I have put this in writing so that posterity may know
the truth and have a record of these events.

"Why should I even mention the spurious letters in which
I am charged with having hoped for Roman liberty? That
fraud would have been exposed had I been permitted to use
the confession of my accusers, the strongest evidence in any
case. But there is now no hope for freedom of any kind—I
only wish there were. I should have answered in the words of
Canius when Gaius Caesar, son f Germanicus,[16] accused
Canius of having known of a co .spiracy against him: 'If I
had known of it,' Canius said, 'yc u would never have known.'
But I am not so discouraged by what has happened to me
that I complain now of the attacks of wicked men against
virtue; the reason for my surprise is that they have accomplished what they set out to do. The desire to do evil may be
due to human weakness; but for the wicked to overcome the
innocent in the sight of God—that is monstrous. I cannot
blame that friend of yours who said, 'If there is a God, why is
there evil? And if there is no God, how can there be good?' [17]
It is not surprising that evil men, who want to destroy all
just men, and the Senate too, should try to overthrow one
who stood up for justice and the Senate. But surely I did not
deserve the same treatment from the Senators themselves.

"You remember well that you always directed me in everything I said and everything I tried to do or say. You recall, for
example, the time at Verona when the King wanted to over-
turn the government and tried to involve the whole Senate

---

[15] Plato, *Theaetetus* 151d and *Republic* 485c.

[16] Gaius Caesar is the Emperor Caligula. (See above, note 8.)

[17] The friend is Epicurus; the quotation is from Lactantius, *De ira Dei*
13. 21.

in the treason of which Albinus was accused; then, at great
risk to my personal safety I defended the innocence of the
whole Senate. You know that this is true, and that I have
never acted out of a desire for praise; for integrity of conscience is somehow spoiled when a man advertises what he
has done and receives the reward of public recognition. But
you see where my innocence has brought me; instead of being
rewarded for true virtue, I am falsely punished as a criminal.
Even the full confession of a crime does not usually make all
the judges in the case equally severe; some, at least, temper
their severity by recognizing the errors of human judgment
and the uncertain conditions of fortune to which all mortals
are subject. If I had been accused of plotting the burning of
churches, the murder of priests, even the murder of all good
men, even then I would have been sentenced only after I had
confessed and been convicted, and when I was present before
the court. But now, five hundred miles away, mute and de-
fenseless, I am condemned to proscription and death because
of my concern for the safety of the Senate. The Senate deserves that no one should ever again be convicted for such a
'crime'!

"Even my accusers understood the honor implicit in the
charges they brought against me, and, in order to confuse the
issue by the appearance of some crime, they falsely alleged
that I had corrupted my conscience with sacrilege out of a
desire for advancement. But your spirit, alive within me, had
driven from my soul all sordid desire for earthly success, and
those whom you protect do not commit sacrilege. You have
daily reminded me of Pythagoras' saying: 'Follow God.' [18] It
is not likely that I would have sought the protection of evil
spirits at a time when you were forming in me that excellence
which makes man like God. Moreover, the innocence of my
family, the honesty of my closest friends, the goodness of my

[18] Boethius gives the Greek ἕπου θεῷ. This saying of Pythagoras is
quoted frequently in classical literature, e.g., Iamblichus, *Vita Pyth.* 18
(86), and Seneca, *De vita beata* 15. 5.

father-in-law,[19] who is as worthy of honor as yourself—all these ought to have shielded me from any suspicion of this crime. But the worst is that my enemies readily believe that wisdom itself is capable of the crime of ambition, and so they associate me with such misconduct because I am imbued with your knowledge and endowed with your virtues. So, my reverence for you is no help; their hatred of me leads them to dishonor you.

"Finally, and this is the last straw, the judgment of most people is based not on the merits of a case but on the fortune of its outcome; they think that only things which turn out happily are good. As a result, the first thing an unfortunate man loses is his good reputation. I cannot bear to think of the rumors and various opinions that are now going around; I can only say that the final misery of adverse fortune is that when some poor man is accused of a crime, it is thought that he deserves whatever punishment he has to suffer. Well, here am I, stripped of my possessions and honors, my reputation ruined, punished because I tried to do good.

"It seems to me that I can see wicked men everywhere celebrating my fall with great pleasure, and all the criminally depraved concocting new false charges. I see good men terrorized into helplessness by my danger, and evil men encouraged to risk any crime with impunity and able to get away with it by bribery. The innocent are deprived not only of their safety, but even of any defense. Now hear my appeal.

Poem 5

Boethius concludes with a prayer.

"Creator of the star-filled universe, seated upon your eternal throne You move the heavens in their swift orbits. You hold the stars in their assigned paths, so that sometimes

[19] Symmachus, also executed by Theodoric. See Introduction, p. x.

the shining moon is full in the light of her brother sun and hides the lesser stars; sometimes, nearer the sun she wanes and loses her glory. You ordain that Hesperus, after rising at nightfall to drive the cold stars before him, should change his role and, as Lucifer, grow pale before the rising sun.[20]

"When the cold of winter makes the trees bare, You shorten the day to a briefer span; but when warm summer comes, You make the night hours go swiftly. Your power governs the changing year: in spring, Zephyrus renews the delicate leaves [21] that Boreas, the wind of winter, had destroyed; and Sirius burns the high corn in autumn that Arcturus had seen in seed.[22]

"Nothing escapes Your ancient law; nothing can avoid the work of its proper station. You govern all things, each according to its destined purpose. Human acts alone, O Ruler of All, You refuse to restrain within just bounds. Why should uncertain Fortune control our lives?

"Harsh punishment, deserved by the criminal, afflicts the innocent. Immoral scoundrels now occupy positions of power and unjustly trample the rights of good men. Virtue, which ought to shine forth, is covered up and hides in darkness, while good men must suffer for the crimes of the wicked. Perjury and deceit are not held blameworthy as long as they are covered by the color of lies. When these scoundrels choose to use their power they can intimidate even powerful kings, because the masses fear them.

"O God, whoever you are who joins all things in perfect harmony, look down upon this miserable earth! We men are no small part of Your great work, yet we wallow here

20 Evening Star (Hesperus) and Morning Star (Lucifer) both signify the planet Venus. Literally the poet says that Hesperus changes his customary reins (i.e., his chariot) to become Lucifer.

21 Zephyrus, the west wind, was said to produce fruits and flowers by his breath.

22 Sirius, the dog-star, supposedly supplied great heat to cause crops to ripen. Arcturus was the brightest star in the constellation Boötes.

in the stormy sea of fortune. Ruler of all things, calm the roiling waves and, as You rule the immense heavens, rule also the earth in stable concord."

PROSE 5

Philosophy suggests that the source of the prisoner's trouble is within himself and begins to reassure him.

While I poured out my long sad story, Philosophy looked on amiably, quite undismayed by my complaints. Then she said: "When I first saw you downcast and crying, I knew you were in misery and exile. But without your story I would not have known how desperate your exile is. You have not been driven out of your homeland; you have willfully wandered away. Or, if you prefer to think that you have been driven into exile, you yourself have done the driving, since no one else could do it. For if you can remember your true country you know that it is not, as Athens once was, ruled by many persons; rather 'it has one ruler and one king,' [23] who rejoices in the presence of citizens, not in their expulsion. To be governed by his power and subject to his laws is the greatest liberty. Surely you know the oldest law of your true city, that the citizen who has chosen to establish his home there has a sacred right not to be driven away.[24] The man who lives within the walls of that city need not fear banishment; but if he loses his desire to live there, he loses also the assurance of safety. And so, I am not so much disturbed by this prison as by your attitude. I do not need your library with its glass walls and ivory decoration, but I do need my place in your mind. For there I have placed not books but that which gives value to books, the ideas which are found in my writings.

"What you have said about your merits in the commonwealth is true; your many services deserve even more than

[23] Homer, *Iliad* II. 204.

[24] Boethius compares the inner security of the philosopher with the civil rights provided by Roman law.

you claim. And what you have said about the truth or falsity of the accusations against you is well known to everyone. You were right to speak sparingly of the crimes and deceit of your enemies; such things are better talked about by the man in the street who hears about them. You have sharply protested the injustice done you by the Senate; and you have expressed sorrow for the accusations against me and the weakening of my place in the public esteem. Finally, you protested against Fortune in sorrow and anger, and complained that rewards are not distributed equally on the grounds of merit. At the end of your bitter poem, you expressed the hope that the same peace which rules the heavens might also rule the earth. But because you are so upset by sorrow and anger, and so blown about by the tumult of your feelings, you are not now in the right frame of mind to take strong medicine. For the time being, then, I shall use more gentle treatment, so that your hardened and excited condition may be softened by gentle handling and thus prepared for more potent remedies.

POEM 6

"The fool who plants his seed in the hard ground when summer burns with the sun's heat [25] must feed on acorns in the fall, because his hope of harvest is in vain. Do not look for violets in purple meadows when fields are blasted by winter winds. And do not cut your vine branches in the spring if you want to enjoy the grapes, for Bacchus brings his fruit in autumn.[26]

"God assigns to every season its proper office; and He does not permit the condition He has set to be altered. Every violent effort to upset His established order will fail in the end.

[25] Literally, "when the sign of Cancer, heavy with the rays of Apollo, burns down."
[26] Bacchus, god of wine.

PROSE 6

Philosophy begins to remind Boethius of certain basic truths which will place his misfortunes in proper perspective.

"First," Philosophy said, "will you let me test your present attitude with a few questions, so that I can decide on a way to cure you?"

"Ask whatever you like," I replied, "and I will try to answer."

"Do you think," she began, "that this world is subject to random chance, or do you believe that it is governed by some rational principle?"

"I cannot suppose that its regular operation can be the result of mere chance; indeed, I know that God the Creator governs his work, and the day will never come when I can be shaken from the truth of this judgment."

"That is true," Philosophy answered, "and you said as much in your poem a while ago when you deplored the fact that only men were outside God's care. You did not doubt that all other things were ruled by reason. Strange, isn't it, that one who has so healthy an attitude should be so sick with despair. We must search further, because obviously something is missing. Tell me, since you have no doubt that the world is ruled by God, do you know *how* it is governed?"

"I don't quite get the point of your question, so I am unable to answer."

"You see, I was right in thinking that you had some weakness, like a breach in the wall of a fort, through which the sickness of anxiety found its way into your soul.

"But tell me, do you remember what the end, or goal, of all things is—the goal toward which all nature is directed?"

"I heard it once," I answered, "but grief has dulled my memory."

"Well, do you know where all things come from?"

I answered that I knew all things came from God.

"How then," she went on, "is it possible that you can know the origin of all things and still be ignorant of their purpose? But this is the usual result of anxiety; it can change a man, but it cannot break him and cannot destroy him.

"I want you to answer this, too: do you remember that you are a man?"

"How could I forget that," I answered.

"Well then, what is a man? Can you give me a definition?"

"Do you mean that I am a rational animal, and mortal? I know that, and I admit that I am such a creature."

"Do you know nothing else about what you are?"

"No, nothing."

"Now, I know another cause of your sickness, and the most important: you have forgotten what you are. And so I am fully aware of the reason for your sickness and the remedy for it too. You are confused because you have forgotten what you are, and, therefore, you are upset because you are in exile and stripped of all your possessions. Because you are ignorant of the purpose of things, you think that stupid and evil men are powerful and happy. And, because you have forgotten how the world is governed, you suppose that these changes of your fortune came about without purpose. Such notions are enough to cause not only sickness but death. But be grateful to the Giver of health that nature has not entirely forsaken you. For you have the best medicine for your health in your grasp of the truth about the way the world is governed. You believe that the world is not subject to the accidents of chance, but to divine reason. Therefore, you have nothing to fear. From this tiny spark, the living fire can be rekindled. But the time has not yet come for stronger remedies. It is the nature of men's minds that when they throw away the truth they embrace false ideas, and from these comes the cloud of anxiety which obscures their vision of truth. I shall try to dispel this cloud by gentle treatment, so that when the darkness of deceptive feeling is removed you may recognize the splendor of true light.

POEM 7

"Stars hidden by black clouds send down no light. If the wild south wind [27] churns up the sea, the waves which once were clear as glass, as clear as the bright days, seem muddy and filthy to the beholder. The flowing stream, tumbling down from the high mountain, is often blocked by the stone broken off from the rocky cliff.

"So it is with you. If you want to see the truth in clear light, and follow the right road, you must cast off all joy and fear. Fly from hope and sorrow. When these things rule, the mind is clouded and bound to the earth."

[27] In the text the south wind is called Auster.

BOOK II

PROSE 1

Philosophy reminds Boethius of the nature and habits of the goddess Fortune.

Philosophy was silent for a while; then, regaining my attention by her modest reserve, she said: "If I understand the causes of your diseased condition, you are suffering from the absence of your former good fortune. What you regard as a change has greatly upset you. I am well acquainted with the many deceptions of that monster, Fortune. She pretends to be friendly to those she intends to cheat, and disappoints those she unexpectedly leaves with intolerable sorrow. If you will recall her nature and habits, you will be convinced that you had nothing of much value when she was with you and you have not lost anything now that she is gone. But I do not suppose that I have to labor this point with you.

"When Fortune smiled on you, you manfully scorned her and attacked her with principles drawn from my deepest wisdom. But every sudden change of fortune brings with it a certain disquiet in the soul; and this is what has caused you to lose your peace of mind. Now is the time for you to take some gentle and pleasant remedy which may prepare you for stronger medicine. I shall use the sweet persuasion of rhetoric, which is suitable enough if it does not contradict the truths of philosophy, and I shall add the grace of Music, a servant of mine whose songs are sometimes happy and sometimes sad.

"What is it, my friend, that has thrown you into grief and sorrow? Do you think that you have encountered something new and different? You are wrong if you think that Fortune has changed toward you. This is her nature, the way she always behaves. She is changeable, and so in her relations with you she has merely done what she always does. This is

21

the way she was when she flattered you and led you on with the pleasures of false happiness. You have merely discovered the two-faced nature of this blind goddess. Although she still hides herself from others, she is now wholly known to you. If you like her, abide by her conditions and do not complain. But if you hate her treachery, ignore her and her deceitful antics. Really, the misfortunes which are now such a cause of grief ought to be reasons for tranquility. For now she has deserted you, and no man can ever be secure until he has been forsaken by Fortune.

"Do you think that your lost happiness is a precious thing? Can present good fortune be dear to you, even though you know that you may lose it, and that the loss will bring sorrow? If you cannot keep her, and if it makes you miserable to lose her, what is fickle Fortune but a promise of future distress? It is not enough to see what is present before our eyes; prudence demands that we look to the future. The double certainty of loss and consequent misery should prevent both the fear of her threats and the desire of her favors. Finally, once you have submitted yourself to her chains, you ought to take calmly whatever she can do to you. If you were to wish for a law to control the comings and goings of one whom you have freely taken for your mistress, you would be unjust and your impatience would merely aggravate a condition which you cannot change. If you hoist your sails in the wind, you will go where the wind blows you, not where you choose to go; if you put seeds in the ground, you must be prepared for lean as well as abundant years.

"You have put yourself in Fortune's power; now you must be content with the ways of your mistress. If you try to stop the force of her turning wheel, you are the most foolish man alive. If it should stop turning, it would cease to be Fortune's wheel.

POEM 1

"When Fortune turns her wheel with her proud right hand, she is as unpredictable as the flooding Euripus; [1] at one moment she fiercely tears down mighty kings, at the next the hypocrite exalts the humbled captive. She neither hears nor cares about the tears of those in misery; with a hard heart she laughs at the pain she causes. This is the way she amuses herself; this is the way she shows her power. She shows her servants the marvel of a man despairing and happy within a single hour.

PROSE 2

Philosophy shows that it is the nature of Fortune to change.

"Let me confront you with the arguments of Fortune herself; then you will see that she is right. She might say to you: 'Why do you bother me with your daily complaints? What have I taken from you that belonged to you? You may argue your case against me before any judge; and if you can prove that riches and honors really belong to any mortal man, I will freely concede your ownership of the things you ask for.

" 'When nature produced you from your mother's womb, I found you naked and lacking in everything. I nourished you with my abundant gifts, and, being inclined to favor you (an attitude which you now seem to hold against me), I endowed you with all the affluence and distinction in my power. Now it pleases me to withdraw my favor. You should be grateful for the use of things which belonged to someone else; you have no legitimate cause for complaint, as though you lost something which was your own. Why then are you so sad? I have done you no injury. Riches, honors, and all

1 Euripus, a narrow strait separating the island of Euboea from the coast of Boeotia, was noted for irregular tides.

good fortune belong to me. They obey me as servants obey their mistress: they come with me, and when I go, they go too. I would even say that, if the things which you complain about losing had really been yours, you would never have lost them.

" 'Why should I alone be deprived of my rights? The heavens are permitted to grant bright days, then blot them out with dark nights; the year may decorate the face of the earth with flowers and fruits, then make it barren again with clouds and frost; the sea is allowed to invite the sailor with fair weather, then terrify him with storms. Shall I, then, permit man's insatiable cupidity to tie me down to a sameness alien to my habits? Here is the source of my power, the game I always play: I spin my wheel and find pleasure in raising the low to a high place and lowering those who were on top. Go up, if you like, but only on condition that you will not feel abused when my sport requires your fall. Didn't you know about my habits? Surely you had heard of Croesus, King of Lydia, who was a formidable adversary to Cyrus at one time and later suffered such reverses that he would have been burnt had he not been saved by a shower from heaven.[2] And you must have heard how Paulus wept over the calamities suffered by Perses, King of Macedonia, whom he captured.[3] What else does the cry of tragedy bewail but the overthrow of happy realms by the unexpected blow of Fortune?

" 'You must have learned as a boy that on Jupiter's doorstep there are two barrels, one holding good things, the other bad.[4] What if you have drawn more abundantly from the barrel of good things? What if I have not deserted you completely? What if my very mutability gives you reason to hope that your fortunes will improve? In any case, do not lose

[2] Croesus, captured by Cyrus, King of Persia, in 548 B.C., was saved from a burning funeral pyre by Apollo who sent a miraculous rain. See Herodotus I. 87.

[3] Amelius Paulus, Consul of Rome, defeated Perses, King of Macedonia, in 168 B.C. See Livy, *Annales* XLV. 7f.

[4] See Homer, *Iliad* XXIV. 527ff.

heart. You live in the world which all men share, so you ought not desire to live by some special law.

POEM 2

" 'If free-handed Plenty should dispense riches from her cornucopia as plentiful as the sands cast up by the storm-tossed sea, or as the stars that shine in heaven on clear nights, men still would not stop crying their miserable complaints.

" 'Even though God were overgenerous with treasures of gold and deigned to satisfy every plea, if He favored the ambitious with the greatest honors, still all this would not satisfy.

" 'Ravenous greed would devour everything and then discover other wants. No bridle can restrain man's disordered desires within reasonable bounds. Even when he is filled with great favors, he burns with thirst for more. No man can be rich who cries fearfully and considers himself to be poor.'

PROSE 3

Philosophy reminds the prisoner of his former prosperity and of the precious gifts he still has.

"If Fortune should argue her case in this way, you would be unable to answer her. But, if you do have something to say in support of your complaint, I will be glad to listen."

"You have made a persuasive argument," I replied, "and presented it with sweet music and rhetoric. But it satisfies only while it is being spoken. Those in misery have a more profound awareness of their afflictions, and therefore a deep-seated pain continues long after the music stops."

"You are quite right," Philosophy answered, "for these words are not supposed to cure your disease but only to kill the pain of your obstinate sorrow. At the proper time I shall apply more deeply penetrating medicine. Still, you ought not to consider yourself completely miserable if you recall your many great joys.

"I will not mention that when you lost your father you were adopted by very prominent people and were chosen to become closely associated with the most powerful figures in the city. You soon were more dear to them by love than you had been close before by relationship, and that is the most precious bond. Everyone considered you most fortunate to have so noble a father-in-law, such a chaste wife, and such fine sons. I pass over such trivial things as the fact that in your youth you received honors which most men never achieve even in old age.

"But I want to stress the greatest of your joys. If any mortal achievement can make a man happy, is it possible that any amount of misfortune can dim the memory of that brilliant occasion when you saw your two sons made Consuls and carried from their house in the company of the Senators and acclaimed by the people? They sat in the Senate in the chairs of consulship while you made a speech in honor of the King which earned high praise for its wit and elegance. You stood between your two honored sons and surpassed the expectations of the great crowd with your triumphant generosity. You pledged yourself to Fortune while she pampered you and favored you with her gifts. You got more from her than any private citizen ever received—and now do you think you can bargain with her?

"This is the first time she ever frowned on you with her evil eye. If you balance the number and kinds of your joys and misfortunes, you must admit that up to now you have been a happy man. If you think yourself unfortunate because you have now lost the things which seemed to make you happy before, still you should not make yourself miserable, because this sorrow will also pass. Do you imagine that you have just come on the stage of life as an unexpected pilgrim? Surely you do not expect to find stability in human affairs, since the life of man himself is often quickly ended. Although it is true that things which are subject to fortune can hardly be counted on, nevertheless, the last day of a man's life is a kind of death to such fortune as he still has. What difference does it make, then, whether you desert her by dying, or she you by leaving?

POEM 3

"When Apollo in his rosy cart begins to spread light across the sky, the stars grow pale and fade before the rushing flame. When the warm west wind blows, the woodland is radiant with spring roses; but the rage of the cold east wind can blast their beauty and leave only thorns. The calm sea often gleams in serene stillness; but often, too, angry storms out of the north throw up huge waves.

"If the form of this world cannot stay the same, but suffers so many violent changes, what folly it is to trust man's tumbling fortunes, to rely on things that come and go. One thing is certain, fixed by eternal law: nothing that is born can last."

PROSE 4

Boethius protests that the worst sorrow is the remembrance of lost joys. Philosophy answers that the only true joy is self-possession in the face of adversity.

Then I answered: "Everything you say is true, dear nurse of all virtues. I do not deny that I came quickly to great prosperity. But the memory of it is what causes me most pain; for in the midst of adversity, the worst misfortune of all is to have once been happy."

"You are being punished for having misjudged your situation," Philosophy answered. "Therefore you have no right to blame the things which bother you. But if you are so impressed by this rather silly notion of happiness based on good fortune, let us consider how very well off you are. Then, if you find that among all the gifts of Fortune your most precious possessions are still safely yours, thanks to God's providence, can you justly complain of misfortune?

"Your father-in-law, Symmachus, one of the finest men who ever lived, and one for whom you would gladly give your life, is still unharmed. That most wise and virtuous man lives in safety to lament the injuries you are suffering. Your wife, so gracious, so chaste, so like her father in excellence of character, still lives, though now she is weary of life and goes on only for your sake. Even I must concede that in her case your happiness is greatly marred since her sorrow for your misfortunes is killing her.

"Think of your sons, the Consuls, who already at their age show the character of their father and grandfather. You are a happy man, if you consider what you still have. The greatest concern of mortals is to preserve life, and you still possess things which everyone agrees are dearer than life itself. So, dry your tears. Fortune has not yet done her worst to you; you have not become a derelict in the storm since those anchors of present comfort and future hope hold fast."

"And I pray that they will continue to hold," I said, "for as long as they do I shall not go down, no matter how bad things get. Still, you see yourself how much I have lost."

"We have made some progress anyway," she answered, "if you have found something to be happy about. But I find your self-pity hard to bear when you moan childishly over the loss of some of your happiness. No one is so completely happy that he does not have to endure some loss. Anxiety is the necessary condition of human happiness since happiness is never completely achieved and never permanently kept. The man who enjoys great wealth may be scorned for his low birth; the man who is honored for his noble family may be oppressed by such poverty that he would rather be unknown. Someone else may enjoy both wealth and social position, but be miserable because he is not married. Still another may be happily married but have no children to inherit his fortune. Others have children, only to be saddened by their vices. Therefore, no one is entirely satisfied with his lot; each finds something lacking, or something which gives pain.

"Besides, those most blessed are often the most sensitive; unless everything works out perfectly, they are impatient at disappointment and shattered by quite trivial things. It takes very little to spoil the perfect happiness of the fortunate. Just think how many people would consider themselves lucky to have only a small part of your remaining good fortune. This very place which you call a land of exile is home to those who live here: nothing is miserable unless you think it so; and on the other hand, nothing brings happiness unless you are content with it. No one is so completely happy that he would not choose to change his condition if he let himself think about it impatiently. The joy of human happiness is shot through with bitterness; no matter how pleasant it seems when one has it, such happiness cannot be kept when it decides to leave.

"You see, then, how shoddy is the enjoyment provided by mortal things. They forsake those who are content with them, and they do not satisfy those who are discontented. Why then do men look outside themselves for happiness which is within? You are confused by error and ignorance and so I will point out to you the source of perfect happiness. Is anything more precious to you than yourself? You will agree that there is nothing. Then if you possess yourself, you have something you will never want to give up and something which Fortune cannot take from you. If you will consider carefully the following argument, you will have to admit that happiness cannot depend on things which are uncertain. If happiness is the highest good of rational natures, and if nothing which can be lost can be a supreme good (because it is obviously less good than that which cannot be lost), then clearly unstable Fortune cannot pretend to bring happiness. The man who enjoys fleeting happiness either knows that it is perishable, or he doesn't. If he does not know it, his condition is unhappy because it rests on blind ignorance; if he knows his happiness is perishable, he must live in fear of losing what he knows can be easily lost—

and such constant fears will not let him be happy. And if he should lose it, would he think that a trivial matter? Whatever can be given up without regret is indeed a thing of little worth. Now, you are a man fully convinced by many proofs that human souls are in no way mortal. It is clear, then, that if transitory happiness ends with the death of the body, and if this means an end of all happiness, the whole human race would be plunged into misery by death. But if we know that many men have sought the enjoyment of happiness not only in death, but also in the sorrows and pains of life, how can this present life make us happy when its end cannot make us unhappy?

POEM 4

"The prudent, steady man who wants a lasting place, immune from blasting winds and dangerous waves, should avoid high mountain peaks and the shore's shifting sands. For the mountain tops are lashed by terrifying gale-winds; and the loose sand of the beach will not bear his weight. Leave then the dangerous places of delight, and make your home safely on the low rocks. Though the wind trouble the sea with threats of destruction, you will live a serene life, happy for having built a strong house in the quiet valley, and laughing at the wrath of the elements.

PROSE 5

Philosophy evaluates the things men strive for and concludes that material possessions bring neither true credit nor safety.

"Now that I see that the soothing medicine of my discourse is taking effect, I think I may risk somewhat stronger remedies. Even if the gifts of Fortune were not momentary and uncertain, there is nothing about them that can ever really be made your own, and they are vile in themselves if you look at them carefully. Are riches naturally precious, or are they precious because of some virtue of yours? What is precious about them, the gold metal or the pile of money? Wealth seems better when it is spent than when it is in the bank, for avarice makes men hated, but liberality makes them popular. But that which is given away is no longer possessed, so that money is more precious when it is generously got rid of. And if all the money in the world were acquired by one man, everyone else would be penniless. The sound of a voice can be given equally to many hearers, but money cannot be distributed among many persons without impoverishing those who give it up. Riches, then, are miserable and troublesome: they cannot be fully possessed by many people, and they cannot be acquired by some without loss to others.

"The brilliance of jewels is eye-catching, but the thing of special value is in the light of the gems rather than in the eye of the beholder. I am amazed that men prize them so highly. For what is there about a thing which lacks the life of the soul and the articulation of the body which can rightly be thought beautiful by human beings who have living, rational natures? It is true that all things derive a certain beauty from the Creator and from their own variety; but they are too far beneath your excellence for you to marvel at them.

"You are, of course, delighted by the beauty of the open fields. And why not, since this is a beautiful part of a very beautiful creation. In the same way we are pleased by a serene sea, we admire the sky, the stars, the sun and the moon; but do any of these things belong to you? How then can you glory in their splendor? You are not adorned with spring flowers, nor are you laden with summer fruit. When you act as though such external goods are your own, you are deluded by foolish satisfaction. Fortune can never make things yours which nature made foreign to you. No doubt the fruits of the earth are given to animals and men for their food; but, if you simply wish to satisfy the demands of nature, there is no reason why you should struggle for the superfluities of Fortune. For nature's needs are few and small; if you try to glut yourself with too many things, you will find your excesses either unpleasant or positively harmful.

"Or perhaps you pride yourself on fine clothes. Well, if they are handsome to look at, I would admire either the quality of the material or the skill of the tailor. Possibly you think that a large number of servants can make you happy. But if they are unreliable or dishonest, they are a pernicious influence in the house and extremely troublesome to their master; on the other hand, if they are good, how can their honesty be considered any virtue of yours?

"Therefore, it ought to be clear that none of these things which you are inclined to take credit for really belong to you. And if there is no desirable beauty in these things, why should you regret losing them, or be particularly elated to possess them? If they are beautiful by nature, what is that to you? They would be pleasing to you even if they belonged to someone else. They are not precious because you have them; you desire to have them because they seem precious.

"What then do you want from Fortune with all your strident demands? I suppose you are trying to avoid poverty by acquiring possessions. But you will find just the opposite: you will need more in order to keep the various valuable things you have. Those who have much, need much; and, on the contrary, those who limit their possessions to their natural needs, rather than to their excessive ambitions, need very little. Do you try to satisfy your desires with external goods which are foreign to you because you have no good within you which belongs to you? What an upside-down state of affairs when a man who is divine by his gift of reason thinks his excellence depends on the possession of lifeless bric-a-brac! Other creatures are content with what they have; but you, made in the likeness of God by virtue of your reason, choose ornaments for your excellent nature from base things, without understanding how great an injury you do to your Creator. God wished the human race to be superior to all earthly things, but you have lowered your dignity below the level of the most trivial things.

For, if it is true that the good thing in which something else finds its good is more precious than the something else which counts it his good, then when you judge vile things to be your goods, you lower yourself beneath them by your own estimate and so deservedly become so. For man is constituted so that when he knows himself he excels all other things; but when he forgets who he is, he becomes worse than the beasts. It is natural for other living things not to know who they are, but in man such ignorance is vice. Your error is painfully evident if you suppose that a man can improve himself by adding ornaments that are not his own. It cannot be done; for if a thing attracts attention by added decoration, that which is added is praised, but that which is covered and disguised remains as base as before.

"Moreover, I deny that anything can be considered good which harms the one who has it. I am sure that you will agree. And riches are frequently harmful to those who possess them. Desperate men are greedy for things that belong to others and think that possession alone is enough to make a man worthy of riches and jewels. Now you are fearful of losing your life; but, if you had walked the road of life as a poor pilgrim, you could laugh in the face of thieves. What a blessing worldly riches are: when you have them, you have lost your safety!

POEM 5 [5]

"Men were most happy in former ages, content with the yield of fertile fields, and not yet ruined by indolent luxury. Their hunger was easily satisfied by acorns. They did not know the potent mixture of wine and honey; they had not learned to color fine silk of Syria with Tyrian dye. They slept soundly on the soft grass, drank from the running streams, and rested in the shade of the high pines.

[5] This poem has long been recognized as a conflation of important commonplace ideas drawn from Virgil's *Georgics,* the first book of Ovid's *Metamorphoses,* and Tibullus.

"Travelers had not yet sailed the high seas to visit foreign ports with their merchandise. Trumpets of war were silent, and blood had not with fierce hate dyed red the gory fields. For how could hostile fury drive men to take up arms when war offered no rewards for gaping wounds except the blood that was spilled?

"Would that our age could return to those ancient virtues; but now man's avarice burns more fiercely than Aetna's fires. Who was he that first dug up the buried gold, the gems that wished to remain hidden, and with them all our costly dangers?

PROSE 6

Philosophy goes on to show that Fortune's gifts of honors and power are transitory and not good in themselves.

"I shall now speak about honors and power which you praise to the sky because you are ignorant of the nature of true honor and power. If these gifts of Fortune are given to a wicked man, they can cause more harm than floods or Aetna's eruptions. Surely, you recall that your ancestors first freed the city from monarchy on account of the pride of kings, and then wanted to abolish consular government, even though it stood for the beginning of their liberty, because of the pride of the consuls. And even in those rare cases when honor and power are conferred upon good men, we are pleased not by the honor and power but by the probity of those who possess them. Thus, honor is not paid to virtuous men because of their rank; on the contrary, it is paid to rank because of the virtue of those holding it.

"What, indeed, is this power which you think so very desirable? You should consider, poor earthly animals, what it is that you seem to have in your power. If you should see a mouse seizing power and lording it over the other mice, how you would laugh! But if you consider only his body, what is weaker than a man who can be killed by the bites of insects or

by worms finding their way into him? For who can force any
law upon man, except upon his body, or upon his fortune
which is less than his body. You can never impose upon a free
spirit, nor can you deprive a rationally self-possessed mind of
its equanimity. Once, when a certain tyrant tried to torture a
free man into betraying the partners of his conspiracy against
the tyrant, the man bit off his tongue and spat it in the raging
tyrant's face.[6] In this way the torments which the tyrant in-
flicted as the means of his cruelty, this wise man made the
means of virtuous action. Indeed, what can any man do to
another which another may not do to him? We recall that
Busirus, who was accustomed to kill his guests, was himself
slain by his guest, Hercules.[7] Regulus had bound many of his
African captives in chains; but before long he was himself
chained by his captors.[8] How slight is the power of a man who
cannot prevent someone else from doing to him what he does
to others.

"Moreover, if honor and power were by nature good in
themselves, they would never be found in wicked men. For
opposites are rarely found together, and nature abhors the
union of contraries. Since there is no doubt that wicked men
are often honored, it is obvious that the kind of honor which
can be achieved by the wicked is not good. And this is even
more obviously the case with all the other gifts of Fortune
which are freely given to vicious men. It may also be said in
this connection that no one doubts the courage of a man in
whom he sees the marks of bravery; nor the swiftness of a man
who obviously can run fast. Similarly, music makes musicians,

6 This story of Anaxarchus, the philosopher, and the tyrant Nicocreon,
King of Cyprus, may be found in Diogenes Laertius IX. 59.

7 Busirus, King of Egypt, used to sacrifice a stranger on the altar of
Zeus once a year. When Hercules was about to be killed in this manner,
he broke his bonds and killed Busirus.

8 Regulus, a Roman consul during the first Punic War, was captured
by the Carthaginians. Sworn by them to negotiate an exchange of pris-
oners, he returned to Rome where, by his own motion in the Senate, the
exchange was refused. Regulus then returned to his captors in Carthage
and was tortured to death by them. See Cicero, *Offices* I. 13.

medical skill makes doctors, rhetoric makes rhetoricians; for each thing does what is proper to its nature. It is not mixed with the characteristics of contrary things; indeed, it repels its opposites. Therefore, riches cannot be separated from insatiable avarice, nor can power make a man master of himself if vicious desires bind him with unbreakable chains. Honor bestowed upon wicked men does not make them honorable; on the contrary, it betrays and emphasizes their dishonor. And why does this happen? It happens because you choose to call things by false names, even though the things in question may be quite different, and the things are then found to contradict their names by their effects. Therefore, material possessions are not rightly called riches, worldly power is not true power, and public honor is not true honor.

"In the end, we reach the same conclusion about all the gifts of Fortune. They are not worth striving for; there is nothing in their natures which is good; they are not always possessed by good men, nor do they make those good who possess them.

POEM 6

"Everyone knows the horrors done by Nero: he burned the city and murdered the Senators; he cruelly killed his own brother, and stained his hands with his mother's blood. He casually looked at her cold body and did not weep, as though he were merely the judge and critic of her dead beauty. Yet this man ruled all the people under the sun from its rising in the east to its setting beneath the waves—all those under the cold northern stars and those scorched by the dry heat of the south winds which roast and burn the hot sands. But all this great power could not subdue the madness of this depraved man. When the evil sword of power is joined to the poison of passion, the commonwealth must groan under an intolerable burden."

PROSE 7

Even the fame won by virtuous men in the performance of honorable public service is of slight value.

Then I said, "You know that ambition for material things has not mastered me; but I have desired the opportunity for public service so that my virtue should not grow old and weak through lack of use."

Philosophy answered, "Indeed, this is the only ambition which can attract minds which are excellent by nature but have not yet achieved perfect virtue. Such minds can be led on by desire for glory and the fame of having deserved well of their commonwealth. But think how trivial and empty such glory is. You know from astrological computation that the whole circumference of the earth is no more than a pinpoint when contrasted to the space of the heavens; in fact, if the two are compared, the earth may be considered to have no size at all. Moreover, as you learned from Ptolemy, only a quarter of this tiny part of the universe is known to be inhabited by living things.[9] And if you mentally subtract from this quarter of the earth all of the area occupied by seas, marshland, and arid deserts, there is almost no space left for human habitation. Do you, therefore, aspire to spread your fame and enhance your reputation when you are confined to this insignificant area on a tiny earth? How can glory be great that is severely limited by such narrow boundaries.

"Then, too, this small inhabited area is occupied by many nations which differ in language, customs, and philosophy of life. Do you suppose that the fame of individual men, or even of cities, can reach nations so remote and different, nations with which there is very little contact? In the time of Cicero,

---

[9] Ptolemy, the famous mathematician, astronomer, and geographer, taught in Alexandria in the middle of the second century. Much of his doctrine, including the idea noted here, was known to the Middle Ages in Macrobius' *Commentary on the Dream of Scipio;* see especially II. 5.

as he says himself somewhere, the fame of the Roman republic had not reached beyond the Caucasus Mountains even though at that period Rome was a mature nation, feared even by the Parthians and others.[10] Do you see now how small and petty the glory is which you strive to extend and increase? Certainly the fame of an individual Roman cannot reach where the fame of Rome herself has not penetrated.

"Moreover, since the customs and institutions of the different nations differ so much, what is praised by some may be condemned by others. The result is that though a man is pleased by the extension of his fame, he is unable to make himself known among many nations. Therefore, a man must be content with a reputation recognized among his own people, since the noble immortality of fame is confined within the boundaries of a single nation.

"Many men who were famous during their lifetime are now forgotten because no one wrote about them. But even written records are of limited value since the long passage of time veils them and their authors in obscurity. When you think about future fame, you imagine that you assure yourselves a kind of immortality. But, if you consider the infinite extent of eternity, what satisfaction can you have about the power of your name to endure? If you compare the duration of a moment with that of ten thousand years, there is a certain proportion between them, however small, since each is limited. But ten thousand years, however many times you multiply it, cannot even be compared to eternity. Finite things can be compared, but no comparison is possible between the infinite and the finite. And so, however long a time fame may last, it must seem not merely brief but nothing at all if it is compared to eternity.

"You mortals, however, know how to act justly only when you have the support of popular opinion and empty rumor; you are not satisfied with the assurance of conscience and virtue but seek your reward in the hollow praise of other men.

[10] See Cicero, *Republic* VI. 22. This sixth book of Cicero's *Republic* was known separately as the *Dream of Scipio*. And see Macrobius' influential *Commentary* II. 10.

Did you ever hear the joke about the folly of such arrogance? One man was ridiculing another who falsely called himself a philosopher; he called himself this not because he practiced true virtue, but because of vanity. The first man claimed that he would find whether or not the other was a philosopher by the way the other humbly and patiently put up with insults. The would-be philosopher bore the insults patiently for a while and then said, 'Now do you think that I am a philosopher?' His tormentor laughed and replied, 'I would have thought so, if you had kept silent.' But seriously, what sort of fame is there for the kind of excellent men I am talking about —those who seek glory through virtue? What do they get from fame after they die? For, if men perish completely in death, a thing which our reason prevents us from accepting, then there is certainly no glory when the man who is supposed to have it no longer exists. But, if the soul, in full awareness of its virtue, is freed from this earthly prison and goes to heaven, does it not disregard all earthly concerns and, in the enjoyment of heaven, find its satisfaction in being separated from earthly things?

POEM 7

"The man who recklessly strives for glory and counts it his highest goal should consider the far-reaching shores of heaven and the narrow confines of earth. He will be ashamed of a growing reputation which still cannot fill so small a space. Why do proud men try in vain to throw this world's burden from their shoulders? Though their fame spread to remote lands and be sung by many voices, though their proud families acquire high honors, still death is contemptuous of such glory and treats the humble and proud in the same manner. Death equalizes the high and the low.

"Where now are the bones of faithful Fabricius? What has become of Brutus and stern Cato? [11] Their slight surviving

---

11 Gaius Fabricius Luscinus, Consul in 282 and 178 B.C., was noted for his austerity and incorruptibility. Lucius Junius Brutus, Consul in 509 B.C.,

fame entrusts their empty names to some few books. But, although we know these fair words, we cannot know the dead. Then lie there, quite unknown, for fame will not keep fresh your memory. If you hope to live on in the glow of your mortal name, the day will come at last to take that too, and you will die a second death.

PROSE 8

Philosophy argues that misfortune is more beneficial than good fortune, for good fortune deceives, but misfortune teaches.

"But do not think that I am engaged in total war with Fortune; for there is a time when that goddess no longer deceives, and then she deserves well of men. That is the time when she unmasks herself, when she shows her face and reveals her true character. But perhaps you do not yet understand what I mean. What I am about to say is so strange that I scarcely know how to make my meaning clear. I am convinced that adverse fortune is more beneficial to men than prosperous fortune. When Fortune seems kind, and seems to promise happiness, she lies. On the other hand, when she shows herself unstable and changeable, she is truthful. Good fortune deceives, adverse fortune teaches. Good fortune enslaves the minds of good men with the beauty of the specious goods which they enjoy; but bad fortune frees them by making them see the fragile nature of happiness. You will notice that good fortune is proud, insecure, ignorant of her true nature; but bad fortune is sober, self-possessed, and prudent through the experience of adversity. Finally, good fortune seduces weak men away from the true good through flattery; but misfortune often turns them around and forcibly leads them back to the true good.

"Do you think it a small matter that your terrible misfortunes have revealed the feelings of those friends who are faith-

was the founder of the Roman Republic. Marcus Porcius Cato (the Greater) was Consul in 195 B.C. He was a model and proponent of strict private and public morality.

ful to you? Fortune has separated your true friends from two-faced ones; when she left you, she took her followers with her and left you your own. Think how much you would have given for this knowledge when you were still on top and thought yourself fortunate. Now you complain of lost riches; but you have found your friends, and that is the most precious kind of wealth.

POEM 8 [12]

"That the universe carries out its changing process in concord and with stable faith, that the conflicting seeds of things are held by everlasting law, that Phoebus in his golden chariot brings in the shining day, that the night, led by Hesperus, is ruled by Phoebe,[13] that the greedy sea holds back his waves within lawful bounds, for they are not permitted to push back the unsettled earth—all this harmonious order of things is achieved by love which rules the earth and the seas, and commands the heavens.

"But if love should slack the reins, all that is now joined in mutual love would wage continual war, and strive to tear apart the world which is now sustained in friendly concord by beautiful motion.

"Love binds together people joined by a sacred bond; love binds sacred marriages by chaste affections; love makes the laws which join true friends. O how happy the human race would be, if that love which rules the heavens ruled also your souls!"

12 This is a classic statement of the medieval idea that love is the principle of harmony in the universe. Divine love established and governs the changing and potentially discordant universe; it should also govern the microcosm, man, in his relations with others. Cf. Book IV, Poem 6.

13 The moon.

BOOK III

Prose 1

Philosophy promises to lead Boethius to true happiness.

When her song was finished, its sweetness left me wondering and alert, eager to hear more. After a while I said, "You are the perfect comforter for weak spirits. I feel greatly refreshed by the strength of your ideas and the sweetness of your music; in fact, I think I may now be equal to the attacks of Fortune. And those remedies you spoke of earlier as being rather harsh —I not only do not fear them, I am quite eager to hear them."

Philosophy answered, "I knew it when I saw you so engrossed, so attentive to what I was saying. I waited for you to achieve this state of mind, or, to put it more truly, I led you to it. You will find what I have yet to say bitter to the taste, but, once you have digested it, it will seem sweet. Even though you say that you want to hear more, your eagerness would be even greater if you knew where I am about to lead you."

"Where?" said I.

"To true happiness, to the goal your mind has dreamed of. But your vision has been so clouded by false images you have not been able to reach it." [1]

"Tell me then," I said. "Show me quickly what true happiness is."

"I will gladly, for your sake. But first I must try to make something else clear, something you know much more about. When you have understood that, you may turn your attention in the opposite direction and then you will be able to recognize the nature of true blessedness.

[1] Cf. Plato, *Republic* 515c.

POEM 1

"The man who wants to sow a fertile field must first clear the ground of brush, then cut out the ferns and brambles with his sharp hook, so that the new grain may grow abundantly.[2]

"Honey is sweeter to the taste if the mouth has first tried bitter flavors. Stars shine more brightly after Notus has stopped his rainy blasts. Only after Hesperus has driven away the darkness does the day drive forward his splendid horses.

"Just so, by first recognizing false goods, you begin to escape the burden of their influence; then afterwards true goods may gain possession of your spirit."

PROSE 2

Philosophy defines the supreme good and the perfect happiness to which all men naturally aspire. She then lists the kinds of false goods which men mistake for the true good.

Philosophy looked away for a moment, as though withdrawn into the sacred chamber of her mind; then she began to speak: "Mortal men laboriously pursue many different interests along many different paths, but all strive to reach the same goal of happiness. Now the good is defined as that which, once it is attained, relieves man of all further desires. This is the supreme good and contains within itself all other lesser goods. If it lacked anything at all, it could not be the highest good, because something would be missing, and this could still be desired. Clearly, then, perfect happiness is the perfect state in which all goods are possessed. And, as I said, all men try by various means to attain this state of happiness; for there is naturally implanted in the minds of men the desire for the true good, even though foolish error draws them toward false goods.

2 The text uses Ceres, goddess of harvest, for grain. Notus, in the paragraph following, is the south wind.

"Some men, believing that the highest good is to have every-thing, exert themselves to become very rich. Others think that the highest good is to be found in the highest honors, and so they try to gain the esteem of their fellow citizens by acquiring various honors. Still others equate the highest good with the greatest personal power. Such men want to be rulers, or at least to associate themselves closely with those in power. Then there are those for whom fame seems the highest good and they labor to spread the glory of their names either in war or in practicing the arts of peace. Others measure the good in terms of gaiety and enjoyment; they think that the greatest happiness is found in pleasure. Finally, there are those who interchange the causes and results of these false goods: some desire riches in order to get power and pleasure; some desire power in order to get money or fame.

"Toward such false goods, and others like them, men direct their actions and desires; they want nobility and popularity, for example, because these seem to bring fame; or they want a wife and children because they regard them as sources of pleas-ure. With regard to friendship, the most sacred kind belongs to the goods of virtue, not of Fortune; all other kinds of friend-ship are sought out of a desire for power or pleasure. At this point it is a simple matter to evaluate the goods of the body in relation to those we have already discussed: size and strength seem to give power; beauty and speed bring fame; health gives pleasure. All this shows clearly that all men seek happiness; for whatever anyone desires beyond all else, he regards as the high-est good. And, since we have defined the highest good as hap-piness, everyone thinks that the condition which he wants more than anything else must constitute happiness.

"You see here practically the whole range of human happi-ness: riches, honor, power, fame, and pleasure. Epicurus, who considered only these possibilities, held pleasure to be the highest good of them all, since the rest seem to bring joy to the soul.[3]

---

[3] Epicurus, *Fragmenta* 348. Cf. St. Augustine, *De civitate Dei* XIX. 1.

"But let me return now to the goals men set for themselves. In spite of its hazy memory, the human soul seeks to return to its true good; but, like the drunken man who cannot find his way home, the soul no longer knows what its good is. Should we consider those men mistaken who try to have everything? Not at all, for nothing can so surely make a man happy as being in full possession of all good things, sufficient in himself and needing no one else. Nor are they mistaken who think that the best men are most worthy of honor, for nothing which nearly all men aspire to achieve can be despised as vile. Power, too, must be considered a good thing, for it would be ridiculous to regard as trivial an asset which can accomplish more than anything else. And what of fame; should we be scornful of it? Surely we must admit that great excellence always carries with it great fame. Finally, it goes without saying that happiness excludes sadness and anguish, that it implies freedom from grief and misery, since even in small things we desire whatever brings delight and enjoyment.

"These, then, are the things which men desire to have: riches, high rank, administrative authority, glory and pleasure, because they believe that these things will give them a good standard of living, honor, power, fame and joy. And whatever men strive for in so many ways must be the good. It is easy to show how strong and natural this striving is because, in spite of the variety and difference of opinion, still all men agree in loving and pursuing the goal of good.

Poem 2

"Now I will show you in graceful song, accompanied by pliant strings, how mighty Nature guides the reins of all things; how she providently governs the immense world by her laws; how she controls all things, binding them with unbreakable bonds.

"The Carthaginian lions endure their fair chains, are fed by hand, and fear the beatings they get from their masters; but if blood should smear their fierce mouths, their sluggish spirits revive, and with a roar they revert to their original nature. They shake off their chains and turn their mad fury on their masters, tearing them with bloody teeth.

"When the chattering bird, who sings in the high branches, is shut up in a narrow cage, she is not changed by the lavish care of the person who feeds her with sweet drink and tasty food. If she can escape from the cramped cage and see the cool shade of the wood, she will scatter the artificial food and fly with yearning to the trees where she will make the forest ring with her sweet voice.

"A treetop bent down by heavy pressure will bow its head to the ground; but if the pressure is released, the tree looks back to heaven again. Phoebus sets at night beneath the Hesperian waves, but returning again along his secret path he drives his chariot to the place where it always rises.

"Thus all things seek again their proper courses, and rejoice when they return to them. The only stable order in things is that which connects the beginning to the end and keeps itself on a steady course.

PROSE 3

Nature inclines men toward the true good, but error deceives them with partial goods. Specifically, riches can never be wholly satisfying.

"You, too, who are creatures of earth, dream of your origin. However weak the vision of your dream may be, you have some vague idea of that goal of true happiness toward which you gaze. Nature leads you toward true good, but manifold error turns you away from it. Consider for a moment whether the things men think can give them happiness really bring them to the goal which nature planned for them. If money, or honor, or other goods of that kind really provide something which seems completely and perfectly good, then I too will admit that men can be happy by possessing them. But, if they not only cannot deliver what they promise, but are found to be gravely flawed in themselves, it is obvious that they have only the false appearance of happiness.

"First, then, since you recently were very rich, let me ask whether or not you were ever worried in spite of your abundant wealth."

"Yes," I answered, "I cannot recall a time when my mind was entirely free from worry."

"And wasn't it because you wanted something you did not have, or had something you did not want?"

"That is true," I answered.

"You wanted this, or didn't want that?"

"Yes."

"Then doesn't everyone lack something that he wants?"

"Yes, he does," I replied.

"And isn't the man who lacks something less than wholly self-sufficient?"

"That is true."

"And even you at the peak of your wealth felt this insufficiency?"

"Of course," I agreed.

"Then wealth cannot give a man everything and make him entirely self-sufficient, even though this is what money seems to promise. But I think it most important to observe that there is nothing in the nature of wealth to prevent its being taken from those who have it."

"That is quite true," I said.

"And why shouldn't you agree, since every day those who are powerful enough snatch it from those who are weaker. In fact, most lawsuits are concerned with efforts to recover money taken by violence or fraud."

I agreed that this was the case.

"Therefore, a man needs the help of others to protect his money."

"Of course."

"But he wouldn't need it, if he had no money to lose."

"There is no doubt about that."

"Well then, the situation is upside down; for riches, which

are supposed to make men self-sufficient, actually make them dependent on the help of others.

"And now let us see whether riches really drive away need. Don't the wealthy become hungry and thirsty; don't they feel cold in the winter? You may argue that they have the means to satisfy their hunger and thirst, and to protect themselves against the cold. Nevertheless, the needs remain, and riches can only minimize them. For if needs are always present and making demands which must be met by spending money, clearly there will always be some need which is unsatisfied. And here I do not press the point that, although nature makes very modest demands, avarice is never satisfied. My present point is simply this: if riches cannot eliminate need, but on the contrary create new demands, what makes you suppose that they can provide satisfaction?

POEM 3

"Though the rich man has a flowing torrent of gold, his avarice can never be fully satisfied. He may decorate his neck with oriental pearls, and plow his fertile lands with a hundred oxen, but biting care will not leave him during life, and when he dies his wealth cannot go with him.

PROSE 4

Honor is not the true good, nor is it the way to true happiness.

"But you may say that high public office makes the man who receives it honorable and worthy of reverence. Do you think that such offices have the power to make those who hold them virtuous and to free them from their vices? On the contrary, public honors usually reveal wickedness rather than correct it, and so we often complain that these honors are given to the worst men. Catullus, for example, called Nonius an ulcer, though he occupied high office.[4] You can see, then, the disgrace that comes to evil men who receive honors. Their unworthiness would be less obvious without the publicity of public recognition. In your own case, could any threats of danger have persuaded you to share public office with Decoratus, once you had found him to be a scoundrel and a spy?[5] We cannot judge men worthy of respect on account of the honors given them, if we find them unworthy of the honors they have received.

"But, if you found a· man distinguished by his wisdom, could you think him unworthy of honor, or of the wisdom which is his?"

"Certainly not," I answered.

"For virtue has its own honor, and this honor is transferred to those who possess virtue. Since popular acclaim cannot accomplish this, clearly it does not have the beauty which is characteristic of true honor. More attention should be paid to this point, for if public contempt makes men abject, public acclaim makes wicked men even more despised since it cannot make them worthy of honor and it exposes them to the world. But public rank itself does not escape untouched, for unworthy men tarnish the offices which they hold by infecting them with their own disease.

"And, to prove further that true honor cannot be attained through these specious dignities, think what would happen if a man who had been many times consul should go to some uncivilized foreign countries. Would the honors which he held at home make him worthy of respect in those places? But, if veneration were a natural part of public honors, it would certainly be given in every nation, just as fire always gives heat wherever it is found in the world. But because popular respect is not a natural consequence of public office, but merely something which depends on untrustworthy public

4 See Catullus LII. 2.

5 Decoratus, a contemporary public official, was Quaestor about the year 508.

opinion, it vanishes when a man finds himself among those who do not regard his position in his home country as a special dignity.

"What I have said so far has to do with the attitudes of foreigners. Do you think that popular acclaim lasts forever among the citizens in the place where it had its origin? The office of praetor once had great power; now it is an empty name and a heavy burden on the treasury of the Senate. The man who in earlier times was responsible for food supply and distribution was counted a great man; now there is no office lower in public esteem. For, as I said before, whatever does not have its own honor in itself, but depends on public whim, is sometimes valued highly, sometimes not at all. Therefore, if public honors cannot make those who have them worthy of reverence, and if, in addition, they are often tainted by the touch of wicked men, and if their value deteriorates with the passage of time, and if they are contemptible in the eyes of foreigners, what desirable beauty do they have in themselves or give to others?

Poem 4

"Although proud Nero in his raging lust adorned himself in Tyrian purple and white pearls, he was hated by all his subjects. But this wicked man once assigned the tainted seats of consulship to venerable men. Who, then, can consider those men blessed who receive their honors from evil men?

Prose 5

Power is not a guarantee of happiness.

"Can royal power, or familiarity with kings, make a man truly powerful? Perhaps, you may say, as long as his happy situation endures. But both the past and the present are full of examples of kings who have fallen from happiness to misery. How wonderful is power which is found incapable even of preserving itself! And even though political power is a cause of happiness, is it not also a cause of misery when it diminishes? Although some human empires extend very widely, there are always some nations which cannot be brought under control; and at the point where power, which makes rulers happy, ends, there the impotence, which makes them miserable, begins. For this reason, rulers have always more misery than happiness. A famous tyrant, who knew the dangers of his position, symbolized the fears of kingship by hanging a drawn sword over the head of a member of his court.[6]

"What, then, is the nature of this power which cannot rid a man of gnawing anxieties nor save him from fear? Those who brag of their power want to live in security, but cannot. Do you consider a person powerful whom you see unable to have what he wants? Do you think a person mighty who is always surrounded by bodyguards, who is more afraid than those whom he intimidates, who puts himself in the hands of his servants in order to seem powerful?

"And what shall I say about the followers of men in power, when the power they attach themselves to is obviously so weak? They can be destroyed by the fall of their leader, or even by his whim while he is still in power. Nero forced his friend and teacher, Seneca, to choose his own manner of execution; Antoninus had Papinianus cut down by the swords of the soldiers, even though he had long been a power among the courtiers.[7] Both of these unfortunate men wanted to give up their power; indeed, Seneca tried to give his wealth to

6 Dionysius the Elder promised to give the flatterer Damocles a taste of the life of a ruler. He placed him in luxurious surroundings and then suspended a sword above his neck. Cf. Cicero, *Tusculan Disputations* V. 21.

7 Papinianus, the Roman jurist, was executed in A.D. 212 after a brilliant career, for disapproving of the emperor's brother.

Nero and retire.[8] But both were destroyed by their very greatness and neither could have what he wanted.

"What, then, is the value of power which frightens those who have it, endangers those who want it, and irrevocably traps those who have it? Are those true friends whom we acquire by fortune rather than virtue? Misfortune will make an enemy of the man whom good fortune made a friend. And what scoundrel is more deadly than one who has been a friend?

POEM 5

"The man who wishes to be powerful must check his desires; he must not permit himself to be overcome by lust, or submit to its foul reins. For even though your rule extends so far that India trembles before you and Ultima Thule [9] serves you, if you cannot withstand black care, and live without wretched moaning, you have no power.

PROSE 6

True happiness is not found in fame.

"As for glory, how deceptive it often is, and how shameful! The tragic playwright justly cries: 'Oh Fame, Fame, how many lives of worthless men you have exalted!' [10] For many men have achieved a great name based on the false opinion of the masses; and what is more disgraceful than that? Those who are falsely praised must blush when they hear the applause. And, even if the praise is merited, what does it matter

[8] See above p. 8, n. 8. In A.D. 62, when Seneca was 70, his relations with Nero were severely strained. The philosopher attempted to retire and give his wealth to Nero, but the emperor refused it. See Tacitus, *Annales* XIV. 54.

[9] Ultima Thule was, to the ancients, the northernmost region of the earth.

[10] Euripides, *Andromache* 319f.

to the wise man who measures his virtue by the truth of his conscience, not by popular esteem. And if it seems a good thing to have widened one's fame, it follows that it must seem a bad thing not to have done so. But since, as I explained earlier, there will always be some countries to which a man's fame does not extend, it follows that the person you think famous will be unknown in some other part of the world.

"In this discussion of fame, I do not think mere popularity even worth mentioning since it does not rest on good judgment, nor has it any lasting life. Moreover, everyone knows that to be called noble is a stupid and worthless thing. If it has anything to do with fame, the fame belongs to others; for nobility appears to be a kind of praise which is really merited by parents. If praise makes a person famous, then those who receive praise are famous; therefore, the praise of others (in this case, of your parents) will not make you famous if you have no fame of your own. In my opinion, therefore, if there is anything to be said for nobility, it lies only in the necessity imposed on the nobility to carry on the virtues of their ancestors.

POEM 6

"The whole race of men on this earth springs from one stock. There is one Father of all things; One alone provides for all. He gave Phoebus his rays, the moon its horns. To the earth He gave men, to the sky the stars. He clothed with bodies the souls He brought from heaven.

"Thus, all men come from noble origin. Why then boast of your ancestors? If you consider your beginning, and God your Maker, no one is base unless he deserts his birthright and makes himself a slave to vice.

PROSE 7

Bodily pleasure cannot make men happy.

"What now shall I say about bodily pleasures? The appetite for them is full of worry, and the fulfillment full of remorse. What dreadful disease and intolerable sorrow, the fruits of wickedness, they bring to the bodies of those who enjoy them! What pleasure there may be in these appetites I do not know, but they end in misery as anyone knows who is willing to recall his own lusts. If they can produce happiness, then there is no reason why beasts should not be called happy, since their whole life is devoted to the fulfillment of bodily needs. The pleasure one finds in his wife and children ought to be a most wholesome thing, but the man who protested that he found his sons to be his torturers spoke what may too often be true. How terrible such a condition can be you must learn from me, since you have never experienced it at first hand, nor do you now suffer from it. In this matter I commend the opinion of Euripides who said that the childless man is happy by his misfortune.[11]

POEM 7

"It is the nature of all bodily pleasure to punish those who enjoy it. Like the bee after its honey is given, it flies away, leaving its lingering sting in the hearts it has struck.

PROSE 8

Philosophy concludes that these limited goods are transitory and cannot bring happiness. On the contrary, they are often positively harmful.

"There is no doubt, therefore, that these are the wrong roads to happiness; they cannot take anyone to the destination

[11] *Ibid.* 420.

which they promise. Let me briefly show you the evils within them. If you try to accumulate money, you must deprive some-one else of it. If you want to cover yourself with honors, you will become indebted to those who can bestow them; and, by wishing to outdo others in honor, you will humiliate your-self by begging.

"If you want power, you risk the danger of your subjects' treachery. If you seek fame, you will become involved in difficulties and lose your security. If you seek a life of pleasure —but who would not spurn and avoid subjection to so vile and fragile a thing as his body? Indeed, those who boast of bodily goods are relying on weak and uncertain possessions. For you are not bigger than an elephant, nor stronger than a bull, nor as quick as a tiger.

"Fix your gaze on the extent, the stability, the swift motion of the heavens, and stop admiring base things. The heavens are not more remarkable in these qualities than in the reason by which they are governed. The beauty of your person passes swiftly away; it is more fleeting than spring flowers. And if, as Aristotle says, men had the eyes of Lynceus and could see through stone walls, would they not find the superficially beautiful body of Alcibiades to be most vile upon seeing his entrails? [12] It is not your nature which makes you seem fair but the weak eyes of those who look at you. You may esteem your bodily qualities as highly as you like as long as you admit that these things you admire so much can be destroyed by the trifling heat of a three-day fever.

"All these arguments can be summed up in the truth that these limited goods, which cannot achieve what they promise, and are not perfect in embracing all that is good, are not man's path to happiness, nor can they make him happy in themselves.

---

[12] This seems to be from a lost work of Aristotle. Lynceus was an Argo-naut whose sight was so sharp that he could distinguish objects more than nine miles away. Alcibiades was a noble Athenian youth noted for his beauty and talent, but also for his arrogance and political dishonesty.

POEM 8

"Alas, what ignorance drives miserable men along crooked paths! You do not look for gold in the green trees, nor for jewels hanging on the vine; you do not set your nets in the high mountains when you want a fish for dinner; nor, if you want to hunt deer, do you seek them along the Tyrenean seas. On the contrary, men are skilled in knowing the hidden caves in the sea, and in knowing where white pearls and scarlet dye are found; they know what beaches are rich in various kinds of fish.

"But, when it comes to the location of the good which they desire, they are blind and ignorant. They dig the earth in search of the good which soars above the star-filled heavens. What can I say to show what fools they are? Let them pursue their riches and honors and, when they have painfully accumulated their false goods, then they may come to recognize the true.

PROSE 9

Philosophy completes her discussion of false happiness and its causes. She then takes up the subject of true happiness and the supreme good.

"Up to this point," said Philosophy, "I have shown clearly enough the nature of false happiness, and, if you have understood it, I can now go on to speak of true happiness."

"I understand well enough," I answered, "that sufficiency is not attained by riches, nor power by ruling others, nor honor by public recognition, nor fame by public acclaim, nor joy by pleasures."

"But have you understood the reasons why this is so?"

"I think I have a vague idea," I said, "but I wish you would show me more plainly."

"The reasons are clear enough. What nature has made simple and indivisible, human error has divided and changed from true and perfect to false and imperfect. Would you say that one who lacks nothing stands in need of power?"

"Of course not."

"You are quite right; for whoever is deficient in any way needs outside help."

"That is true," I said.

"Therefore, sufficiency and power have one and the same nature."

"That seems to be true."

"And would you say that a thing which is perfectly self-sufficient and completely powerful should be scorned, or is it, on the contrary, worthy of honor?"

"Undoubtedly it is most worthy of honor."

"Then we may add reverence to sufficiency and power, and conclude that all three are really one."

"That is true."

"Next, would you think such a thing obscure and base, or rather, famous and renowned? Now think for a moment whether that which is conceded to be self-sufficient, all powerful, and worthy of great reverence can stand in need of any fame which it cannot give to itself, and therefore seem in some way defective."

"I confess that being what it is it must also be famous."

"It follows, then, that fame cannot be separated from the other three."

"That is true."

"Therefore, that which is self-sufficient, which can do everything by its own power, which is honored and famous, is not this also most pleasant and joyful?"

"I cannot imagine how anyone possessing all these attributes could be sad; and so, if the argument thus far is sound, I must confess that this thing must also be joyful."

"Then," Philosophy went on, "it must be granted that, although the names of sufficiency, power, fame, reverence, and joy are different, in substance all are one and the same thing."

"That must be granted," I agreed.

"Human depravity, then, has broken into fragments that which is by nature one and simple; men try to grasp part of a thing which has no parts and so get neither the part, which does not exist, nor the whole, which they do not seek."

"How is this?" I asked.

"The man who seeks wealth in order to avoid poverty is not interested in power; he would rather be obscure and weak and will even deprive himself of many natural pleasures so that he won't lose the money he has collected. But such a man does not even acquire sufficiency; he is powerless, plagued by trouble, held in contempt, and hidden in obscurity. Similarly, the man who seeks only power wastes his money, scorns pleasures and honors that carry with them no power, and thinks nothing of fame. But see how much he is missing: sometimes he is without the necessities of life, he is plagued by anxieties, and when he cannot overcome them he loses that which he wants most—he ceases to be powerful. Honors, fame, and pleasure can be shown to be equally defective; for each is connected with the others, and whoever seeks one without the others cannot get even the one he wants."

"What happens when someone tries to get them all at the same time?" I asked.

"He, indeed, reaches for the height of happiness, but can he find it in these things which, as I have shown, cannot deliver what they promise?"

"Of course not," I said.

"Happiness, then, is by no means to be sought in these things which are commonly thought to offer the parts of what is sought for."

"Nothing can be truer than this," I agreed.

"Now you have grasped the nature of false happiness and its causes. Now turn your mind's eye in the opposite direction and there you will see the true happiness which I promised to show you."

"But this is clear even to a blind man," I said, "and you revealed it a little while ago when you tried to explain the causes of false happiness. For, unless I am mistaken, true and perfect happiness is that which makes a man self-sufficient, powerful, worthy of reverence and renown, and joyful. And, to show that I have understood you, I acknowledge that whatever can truly provide any one of these must be true and perfect happiness, since all are one and the same."

"O, my scholar," Philosophy answered, "your observation is a happy one if you add just one thing."

"What is that?" I asked.

"Do you imagine that there is any mortal and frail thing which can bring about a condition of this kind?"

"Not at all," I said, "but I think you have proved that beyond any need for further discussion."

"Then these false causes of happiness are mere appearances of the true good and merely seem to give certain imperfect goods to mortal men; but they cannot give true and perfect good."

"I agree," I said.

"Now then, since you know what true happiness is, and the things that falsely seem to offer it, you must now learn where to look for true happiness."

"This," I answered, "is what I have eagerly looked forward to."

"But since, as Plato says in his *Timaeus*,[13] we ought to implore divine help even in small things, what do you think is called for now if we are to gain access to the throne of the highest good?"

"We must invoke the Father of all things without whose aid no beginning can be properly made."

"You are right," said Philosophy, and she began to sing this song:

13 *Timaeus* 27c.

POEM 9 [14]

"Oh God, Maker of heaven and earth, Who govern the world with eternal reason, at your command time passes from the beginning. You place all things in motion, though You are yourself without change. No external causes impelled You to make this work from chaotic matter. Rather it was the form of the highest good, existing within You without envy, which caused You to fashion all things according to the eternal exemplar. You who are most beautiful produce the beautiful world from your divine mind and, forming it in your image, You order the perfect parts in a perfect whole.

"You bind the elements in harmony so that cold and heat, dry and wet are joined, and the purer fire does not fly up through the air, nor the earth sink beneath the weight of water.

"You release the world-soul throughout the harmonious parts of the universe as your surrogate, threefold in its operations, to give motion to all things.[15] That soul, thus divided, pursues its revolving course in two circles, and, returning to itself, embraces the profound mind and transforms heaven to its own image.

"In like manner You create souls and lesser living forms and, adapting them to their high flight in swift chariots, You scatter them through the earth and sky. And when they

[14] This remarkable philosophical poem is an epitome of the first part of Plato's *Timaeus*. The poem was widely used and commented on in the Middle Ages.

[15] A difficult and ambiguous sentence. The text is: "Tu triplicis medium naturae cuncta moventem / connectens animam per consona membra resolvis" (II. 13-14). I have rendered *triplicis naturae* as modifying *animam*, "the world-soul . . . threefold in its operations," because this is the reading of Boethius' early medieval commentators. The idea that nature itself is threefold, "the soul of threefold nature," is also supported by historical evidence. Given the relation between the world-soul and nature the difference between these readings is not crucial to Boethius' statement here.

have turned again toward You, by your gracious law, You call them back like leaping flames.

"Grant, Oh Father, that my mind may rise to Thy sacred throne. Let it see the fountain of good; let it find light, so that the clear light of my soul may fix itself in Thee. Burn off the fogs and clouds of earth and shine through in Thy splendor. For Thou art the serenity, the tranquil peace of virtuous men. The sight of Thee is beginning and end; one guide, leader, path, and goal.

Prose 10

Philosophy teaches Boethius that the supreme good and highest happiness are found in God and are God.

"Since you have seen the forms of imperfect and perfect good, I think it is now time to show where this perfection of happiness resides. First, we must ask whether a good of the kind you defined a short while ago can exist at all, so that we may not be deceived by an empty shadow of thought and thus be prevented from reaching the truth of our problem. Now, no one can deny that something exists which is a kind of fountain of all goodness; for everything which is found to be imperfect shows its imperfection by the lack of some perfection. It follows that if something is found to be imperfect in its kind, there must necessarily be something of that same kind which is perfect. For without a standard of perfection we cannot judge anything to be imperfect. Nature did not have its origins in the defective and incomplete but in the integral and absolute; it fell from such beginnings to its present meanness and weakness.

"But if, as I have just pointed out, there is a certain imperfect happiness in transitory goods, no one can doubt that there is a perfect and enduring happiness."

"That is firmly and truly established," I said.

"Now consider where this perfect happiness has its dwelling place. It is the common conception of the human mind that

God, the ruler of all things, is good. For, since nothing can be thought of better than God, who can doubt that He is the good, other than whom nothing is better. And that God is good is demonstrated by reason in such a way as to convince us that He is the perfect good. If He were not, He could not be the ruler of all things; for there would be something better than He, something possessing perfect good, which would seem to be older and greater than He. For all perfect things have been shown to come before less perfect ones. And so, if we are to avoid progression *ad infinitum,* we must agree that the most high God is full of the highest and most perfect good. But we have already established that perfect good is true happiness; therefore it follows that true happiness has its dwelling in the most high God."

"I agree," I said. "Your argument cannot be contradicted."

"But observe," Philosophy continued, "how you may prove scrupulously and inviolably what I have just said, namely, that the most high God is full of the highest good."

"How?" I asked.

"By avoiding the notion that the Father of all things has received from others the highest good with which He is filled, or that He has it naturally in such a way that He and the happiness which He has may be said to differ in essence. For, if you should suppose that He receives it from someone else, you could think that the one who gives it is greater than the one who receives it; but we worthily confess that God is the most excellent of all beings. And if He has this happiness by nature, but differs from it, then someone else who can will have to explain how these diverse things are joined together, since we are speaking of God the Creator of all things. Finally, that which is different from anything cannot be the thing from which it differs; therefore, that which according to its nature differs from the highest good cannot be the highest good. But it is blasphemous to think this about One other than whom, as we know, nothing is greater. And surely there can be nothing better by nature than its source; therefore, I may conclude with certainty that whatever is the source of all things must be, in its substance, the highest good."

"I agree."

"And do you also agree that the highest good is happiness?"

"Yes."

"Then," said Philosophy, "you must agree that God is happiness."

"I found your earlier arguments unassailable, and I see that this conclusion follows from them."

"Then consider whether the same conclusion is not even more firmly established by this, that there cannot exist two highest goods which differ from one another. Clearly, when two goods differ, one cannot be the other; therefore, neither can be perfect since it lacks the other. But that which is not perfect certainly cannot be the highest good; therefore, those things which are the highest good cannot be diverse. But I have proved that happiness and God are the highest good; therefore, that must be the highest happiness which is the highest divinity."

"I can think of nothing truer, or more reasonable, or worthier of God," I said.

"From this conclusion, then, I will give you a kind of corollary, just as the geometricians infer from their demonstrated propositions things which they call deductions. Since men become happy by acquiring happiness, and since happiness is divinity itself, it follows that men become happy by acquiring divinity. For as men become just by acquiring integrity, and wise by acquiring wisdom, so they must in a similar way become gods by acquiring divinity. Thus everyone who is happy is a god and, although it is true that God is one by nature, still there may be many gods by participation."

"This is a beautiful and precious idea," I said, "whether you call it a corollary or a deduction."

"And there is nothing more beautiful," Philosophy went on, "than the truth which reason persuades us to add to this."

"What is that?" I asked.

"Since happiness seems composed of many things, would you say that all these are joined together in happiness, as a variety of parts in one body, or does one of the parts constitute the essence of happiness with all the rest complementing it?"

"I wish you would explain this point by recalling what is involved."

Philosophy then continued. "Do we not agree that happiness is good?"

"Indeed, it is the highest good," I replied.

"Then we must add this good to all the others; for happiness is considered the fullest sufficiency, the greatest power, honor, fame, and pleasure. Now are all these to be regarded as good in the sense that they are members or parts of happiness, or are they simply related to the good as to their crown?"

"I understand the problem now and am eager to have your answer."

"Here then is the solution. If all these goods were constituent parts of happiness, each would differ from the others; for it is the nature of parts to be different things constituting one body. But I have proved that all these goods are one and the same thing; therefore they cannot be parts. Otherwise, happiness would seem to be constituted of one part, which is a contradiction in terms."

"There is no doubt about that," I said, "but you have not yet given me the solution."

"Clearly, all the rest must be related to the good. For riches are sought because they are thought good, power because it is believed to be good, and the same is true of honor, fame, and pleasure. Therefore, the good is the cause and sum of all that is sought for; for if a thing has in it neither the substance nor the appearance of good, it is not sought or desired by men. On the other hand, things which are not truly good, but only seem to be, are sought after as if they were good. It follows, then, that goodness is rightly considered the sum, pivot, and cause of all that men desire. The most important object of desire is that for the sake of which something else is sought as a means; as, for example, if a person wishes to ride horseback in order to improve his health, he desires the effect of health more than the exercise of riding.

"Since, therefore, all things are sought on account of the good, it is the good itself, not the other things, which is desired by everyone. But, as we agreed earlier, all those other things are sought for the sake of happiness; therefore, happiness alone is the object of men's desires. It follows clearly from this that the good and happiness are one and the same thing."

"I cannot see how any one could disagree."

"But we have also proved that God and true happiness are one and the same."

"That is so."

"We can, therefore, safely conclude that the essence of God is to be found in the good, and nowhere else.

POEM 10 [16]

"Come, all you who are trapped and bound by the foul chains of that deceiving lust which occupies earth-bound souls. Here you will find rest from your labors, a haven of steady quiet, a refuge from misery.

"Nothing that the river Tagus with its golden shores can give, nor the Hermus with its jeweled banks, the Indus of the torrid zone, gleaming with green and white stones, none of these can clear man's vision. Instead, they hide blind souls in their shadows.

"Whatever pleases and excites your mind here, Earth has prepared in her deep caves. The shining light which rules and animates the heavens avoids the dark ruins of the soul. Whoever can see this light will discount even the bright rays of Phoebus."

16 With the discussions of the nature of the Good in this poem and the following prose section, compare Boethius' treatment of the same subject in his theological treatise *Quomodo substantiae*, Loeb Classical Library, pp. 38ff.

PROSE 11

Philosophy shows that God is One and that He is the goal toward which all things tend.

"I must agree, since your entire argument is established by sound reasons."

"Then," Philosophy continued, "how highly would you value it, if you could know what the absolute good is?"

"Such knowledge would be of infinite value," I said, "if I were also able to know God who is the absolute good."

"Well, I will show you this with certainty, if the conclusions we have arrived at so far are correct."

"They are indeed," I said.

"I have already proved that the things which most people want are not the true and perfect good since they differ from one another; and, since one or the other is always missing, they cannot provide full and perfect good. But I have also shown that they become the true good when they are gathered together as it were into a single form and operation, so that sufficiency becomes the same as power, honor, fame, and pleasure. And I have further shown that unless they are all one and the same, there is no reason to consider them desirable."

"You have proved this beyond doubt."

"Therefore, if these partial goods cannot be truly good if they are different, but are good if they become one, then clearly they become good by acquiring unity."

"This seems to be true," I said.

"But, if you also grant that every good is good by participating in the perfect good, then you should concede by a similar line of reasoning that the good and the one are the same. For things are of the same essence if their effects are of the same nature."

"I cannot deny that."

"And do you also understand that everything that is remains and subsists in being as long as it is one; but that when it ceases to be one it dies and corrupts?"

"How is this?"

"In the case of animals, when body and spirit are joined together in one being and remain so, that being is called a living thing; but when this unity is dissolved by the separation of body and soul, the being dies and is no longer a living animal. Even the body seems to be human as long as it remains one form in the union of its members; but, if this unity is broken by the separation and scattering of the body's members, it ceases to be what it was before. If we go on to examine other things we will see that each has its being as long as it is one, but when it begins to lose that oneness, it dies."

"On further consideration, I see that this is so."

"Is there anything, then, which acting naturally, gives up its desire to live and chooses to die and decay?"

"When I consider animals whose natures give them some choice, I know of none which gives up the will to live and of its own accord seeks death as long as it is free of external pressure. For every living being acts to preserve its life and to avoid death and injury. But, about plants and trees and inanimate objects, I simply do not know."

"You should not be in doubt about them, since you observe that trees and plants take root in suitable places and, to the extent made possible by their natures, do not wither and die. Some grow in the fields, some in the mountains, some in marshland, some in rocky places, some flourish in the sterile sands; but if any of these should be transplanted to some other place, they would die. Nature gives all things what they need and takes care that they live as long as they can. Why do all plants get their nourishment from roots, like a mouth drinking from the ground, and build up rugged bark over the pith? Why is the soft substance on the inside, while on the outside is the firm wood, and covering all is the bark, a rugged defender against harm, protecting the plant against storms? Note, too, how diligent nature is in propagating every species by multiplying the seed. Everyone knows that these natural processes are designed for the permanent preservation of the species as well as for the present life of individual plants.

"Even things believed to be inanimate do what is proper to their natures in much the same way. Why does lightness cause flames to rise and weight cause earth to settle, if not that these phenomena are appropriate to the things concerned? In addition, each thing is kept in being by that which is naturally proper to it, just as each thing is corrupted by that which is naturally opposed to it. Hard things, such as stones, resist fragmentation by the tough cohesion of their parts; but fluid things, such as air and water, are easily parted, but then quickly flow together again; fire, however, cannot be cut at all. We are not concerned here with the voluntary motions of the intelligent soul, but only of those natural operations of which we are unconscious, such as, for example, digestion of food and breathing during sleep. Indeed, even in living beings, the desire to live comes not from the wishes of the will but from the principles of nature. For often the will is driven by powerful causes to seek death, though nature draws back from it. On the other hand, the work of generation, by which alone the continuation of mortal things is achieved, is sometimes restrained by the will, even though nature always desires it. Thus, this love for the self clearly comes from natural instinct and not from voluntary activity. Providence gave to his creatures this great urge for survival so that they would desire to live as long as they naturally could. Therefore you cannot possibly doubt that everything which exists naturally desires to continue in existence and to avoid harm."

"I now see clearly," I said, "what up to now seemed uncertain."

"Furthermore," Philosophy went on, "whatever seeks to exist and endure also desires to be one; for without unity existence itself cannot be sustained."

"That is true," I said.

"Then all things desire unity."

I agreed.

"But I have already shown that unity is the same as goodness."

"True," I said.

"Therefore, all things desire the good, so that we can define the good as that which is desired by all."

"That is perfectly correct," I agreed. "For either there is no one thing to which all other things are related, and therefore they wander without direction or goal, or, if there is something toward which all things hasten, it is the highest of all goods."

"I am greatly pleased with you, my pupil, for you have found the key to truth. And you also see clearly what a while ago you said you did not understand."

"What is that?" I asked.

"The end, or goal, of all things. For surely it is that which is desired by all; and, since we have identified that as the good, we must conclude that the good is the end toward which all things tend.

POEM 11

"The man who searches deeply for the truth, and wishes to avoid being deceived by false leads, must turn the light of his inner vision upon himself. He must guide his soaring thoughts back again and teach his spirit that it possesses hidden among its own treasures whatever it seeks outside itself.

"Then all that was hidden by the dark cloud of error will shine more clearly than Phoebus; for the body, with its burden of forgetfulness, cannot drive all light from his mind. The seed of truth grows deep within and is roused to life by the breath of learning. For how can you answer questions truly unless the spark of truth glows deep in your heart? If Plato's Muse speaks truly, whatever is learned is a recollection of something forgotten." [17]

[17] Plato's theories of reminiscence may be found in *Phaedo* 72-76.

PROSE 12

Philosophy shows that God rules the universe by his goodness and that all created things obey him.

"I agree fully with Plato," I said, "for this is the second time I have been reminded of these truths. I forgot them first under the oppressive influence of my body, then later when I was depressed by grief."

Philosophy replied, "If you consider carefully the conclusions you have so far granted, you will quickly remember something else which you said a while ago that you did not know."

"What is that?"

"The way the world is governed," she said.

"I do remember confessing my ignorance about that," I answered, "and, even though I can now anticipate your answer, I want to hear it plainly from you."

"Earlier in our discussion," Philosophy said, "you affirmed without any doubt that the world is ruled by God." [18]

"I still have no doubt about it, and never will, for these reasons: this world could never have achieved its unity of form from such different and contrary parts unless there were One who could bring together such diverse things. And, once this union was effected, the very diversity of discordant and opposed natures would have ripped it apart and destroyed it, if there were not One who could sustain what He had made. Nor could the stable order of nature continue, nor its motions be so regular in place, time, causality, space and quality, unless there were One who could govern this variety of change while remaining immutable Himself. This power, whatever it may be, by which created things are sustained and kept in motion, I call by the name which all men use, God." [19]

Philosophy answered, "Since this is your conviction, I think it will be easy to restore your happiness and bring you back

[18] See Book I, Prose 6 and Book III, Poem 9.

[19] Compare Boethius' treatment of creation in the theological treatise *De fide Catholica*, Loeb Classical Library, pp. 56ff.

safely to your own country. Now let us return to our task. Have we not already shown that sufficiency is among the attributes of happiness, and are we not agreed that God is absolute happiness?"

"That is right," I said.

"Then He needs no outside help in ruling the world; otherwise, if He were in need of anything He would not be completely self-sufficient."

"That is necessarily true," I said.

"Therefore He disposes all things by himself alone."

"I agree."

"Moreover, I have proved that God is absolute good."

"I remember that," I said.

"Then if He, whom we have agreed to be the good, rules all things by himself, He must dispose everything according to the good. He is, in a manner of speaking, the wheel and rudder by which the vessel of the world is kept stable and undamaged."

"I fully agree," I said, "and I saw in advance, though somewhat vaguely, that this is what you would say."

"I don't doubt it," Philosophy replied, "for I think that you are now looking more sharply for the truth. But what I am now going to tell you is equally clear."

"What is that?" I asked.

"Since God is rightly believed to govern all things with the rudder of goodness, and since all these things naturally move toward the good, as I said earlier, can you doubt that they willingly accept His rule and submit freely to His pleasure as subjects who are agreeable and obedient to their leader?"

"This must be so," I answered, "for no rule could be called happy if it were a bondage of willing slaves rather than one designed for the welfare of compliant citizens."

"Then there is nothing which, by following nature, strives to oppose God?"

"Nothing," I agreed.

"And, if anything should try to oppose Him, could it be at all successful against the One we have rightly shown to be the supreme power of happiness?"

"It would have no chance whatever," I said.

"Then there is nothing which has either the desire or the power to oppose this highest good?"

"Nothing."

"Then it is the supreme good which rules all things firmly and disposes all sweetly."

"I am delighted," I said, "not only by your powerful argument and its conclusion, but even more by the words you have used. And I am at last ashamed of the folly that so profoundly depressed me."

"You have read in the fables of the poets how giants made war on heaven; but this benign power overthrew them as they deserved. But now let us set our arguments against each other and perhaps from their opposition some special truth will emerge."

"As you wish," I said.

"No one can doubt that God is almighty," Philosophy began.

"Certainly not, unless he is mad," I answered.

"But nothing is impossible for one who is almighty."

"Nothing."

"Then can God do evil?"

"No, of course not."

"Then evil is nothing, since God, who can do all things, cannot do evil."

"You are playing with me," I said, "by weaving a labyrinthine argument from which I cannot escape. You seem to begin where you ended and to end where you began. Are you perhaps making a marvelous circle of the divine simplicity? A little while ago you began with happiness, declared it to be the highest good, and located its dwelling in almighty God. You said that God himself is the highest good and perfect happiness. From this you inferred that no one could be happy unless he too were a god. Then you went on to say that the very form of the good is the essence of God and of happiness; and you said further that unity is identical with the good which is sought by everything in nature. You also affirmed that God rules the universe by the exercise of His goodness, that all things willingly obey Him, and that there is no evil in nature. And you proved all this without outside assumptions and used only internal proofs which draw their force from one another."

Philosophy answered, "I have not mocked you at all. With the help of God whose aid we invoked we have reached the most important point of all. For it is the nature of the divine essence neither to pass to things outside itself nor to take any external thing to itself. As Parmenides puts it, the divine essence is 'in body like a sphere, perfectly rounded on all sides'; [20] it rotates the moving orb of the universe while it remains unmoved itself. You ought not to be suprised that I have sought no outside proofs, but have used only those within the scope of our subject, since you have learned, on Plato's authority, that the language we use ought to be related to the subject of our discourse.[21]

POEM 12

"Happy is he who can look into the shining spring of good; happy is he who can break the heavy chains of earth.

"Long ago the Thracian poet, Orpheus, mourned for his dead wife. With his sorrowful music he made the woodland dance and the rivers stand still. He made the fearful deer lie down bravely with the fierce lions; the rabbit no longer feared the dog quieted by his song.

"But as the sorrow within his breast burned more fiercely, that music which calmed all nature could not console its maker. Finding the gods unbending, he went to the regions of hell. There he sang sweet songs to the music of his harp, songs drawn from the noble fountains of his goddess mother, songs inspired by his powerless grief and the love which doubled his grief.

"Hell is moved to pity when, with his melodious prayer,

[20] Parmenides, *Fragment* VIII. 43.
[21] *Timaeus* 29b.

he begs the favor of those shades. The three-headed guardian of the gate is paralyzed by that new song; and the Furies, avengers of crimes who torture guilty souls with fear, are touched and weep in pity. Ixion's head is not tormented by the swift wheel, and Tantalus, long maddened by his thirst, ignores the waters he now might drink. The vulture is filled by the melody and ignores the liver of Tityus.

"At last, the judge of souls, moved by pity, declares, 'We are conquered. We return to this man his wife, his companion, purchased by his song. But our gift is bound by the condition that he must not look back until he has left hell.' But who can give lovers a law? Love is a stronger law unto itself. As they approached the edge of night, Orpheus looked back at Eurydice, lost her, and died.

"This fable applies to all of you who seek to raise your minds to sovereign day. For whoever is conquered and turns his eyes to the pit of hell, looking into the inferno, loses all the excellence he has gained."

BOOK IV

PROSE 1

Boethius wonders about the existence, and apparent success, of evil in the world created and ruled by God.

Philosophy told the story of Orpheus softly and sweetly, with her customary dignity. When she had finished, and seemed about to continue her discourse, I broke in, still depressed by my personal grief.

"O guide to true light, all that you have so far told me is divine in itself and perfectly convincing by virtue of your argument. But, although the sorrow caused by my misfortunes had made me forget these truths, I had not always been ignorant of them. Here, though, is the greatest cause of my sadness: since there is a good governor of all things, how can there be evil, and how can it go unpunished. Think how astonishing this is. But it is even more amazing that with wickedness in full control, virtue not only goes unrewarded, but is trampled underfoot by the wicked and is punished instead of vice. That this can happen in the realm of an all-knowing and all-powerful God who desires only good must be a cause of surprise and sorrow to everyone."

Philosophy answered, "It would indeed be a monstrous thing and astonishing to everyone if, as you suppose, in the well-ordered house of so great a father the vilest objects were cherished and the most precious were regarded with contempt. But this is not the case. For if our previous conclusions are valid, and with the help of Him whose kingdom we are now speaking of, you will discover that the good are always powerful and the evil always weak and futile, that vice never goes unpunished nor virtue unrewarded, that the good prosper and the evil suffer misfortune, and much else which will remove the causes of your complaint and strengthen your convictions.

75

And since under my guidance you have understood the essence of true happiness, and have found out where it resides, I shall now run through the steps in my explanation which I think necessary and show you the path which will take you home. And I shall give wings to your mind which can carry you aloft, so that, without further anxiety, you may return safely to your own country under my direction, along my path, and by my means.

POEM 1

"My wings are swift, able to soar beyond the heavens. The quick mind which wears them scorns the hateful earth and climbs above the globe of the immense sky, leaving the clouds below. It soars beyond the point of fire caused by the swift motion of the upper air until it reaches the house of stars. There it joins Phoebus in his path, or rides with cold, old Saturn, companion of that flashing sphere, running along the starry circle where sparkling night is made. When it has seen enough, it flies beyond the farthest sphere to mount the top of the swift heaven and share the holy light.

"There the Lord of kings holds His scepter, governing the reins of the world. With sure control He drives the swift chariot, the shining judge of all things.

"If the road which you have forgotten, but now search for, brings you here, you will cry out: 'This I remember, this is my own country, here I was born and here I shall hold my place.' Then if you wish to look down upon the night of earthly things which you have left, you will see those much feared tyrants dwelling in exile here."

PROSE 2

Philosophy shows that the good have true power and the vicious do not.

Hearing this I said, "What wonderful things you promise! And I have no doubt that you can do them. But do not hold me in suspense now that you have made me so eager."

"First," Philosophy answered, "you will agree that the good always have power and the wicked do not. Each of these propositions proves the other: for, since good and evil are contraries, if good is shown to be powerful, the weakness of evil necessarily follows. Conversely, if evil is shown to be weak, the strength of good is clear. But, in order to demonstrate this truth fully, I will prove my point in both ways one after the other.

"The success of any human action depends upon two things: will and power. If either is lacking nothing can be done. If the will is absent, nothing is attempted; if power is lacking, the will is frustrated. Therefore, if you find someone wanting something and not getting it, you must conclude that he is without the power to obtain what he wants."

"That is quite clear," I said, "and no one can deny it."

"On the other hand, you will agree that the man who gets what he wants had the power to get it."

"That is equally clear."

"Moreover, whatever a man can do, he has the power to do; but what he cannot do shows lack of power."

"That is true," I agreed.

"Then do you recall that earlier in our discussion we found that every intention of the human will is directed toward happiness, however various its inclinations may be?"

"I remember that to have been proved."

"And do you also recall that happiness is the good, so that everyone who seeks happiness also desires the good?"

"I have not forgotten," I said. "Indeed, I hold it fast in my memory."

"Therefore, all men, good and bad, have the same purpose in striving to obtain the good."

"That follows," I agreed.

"But it is also true that men become good by obtaining the good."

"Yes."

"So good men obtain what they desire."

"That seems to be true."

"But evil men would not be evil if they obtained the good they seek."

"That is true."

"Therefore, since both seek the good, but good men obtain it and evil men do not, it follows that good men have power but evil men are impotent."

"To doubt that would be to disregard the nature of things and the force of argument."

"Next," Philosophy continued, "suppose that there are two persons to whom the same natural function is assigned: one of them accomplishes the action by natural means, but the other is unable to do so and uses unnatural means, not indeed to accomplish the action but to pretend to do so. Which of these two would you consider the more powerful?"

"I think I see what you are driving at, but please explain more fully."

"Well, you will agree that the act of walking is natural for men, and that the feet are the natural means of accomplishing the action."

"Quite so."

"Then if one man is able to walk on his feet, and another, who is deprived of this natural capability, tries to walk by crawling on his hands, which of the two must rightly be thought the stronger?"

"That goes without saying," I answered, "for everyone knows that the man who can use his natural capacities is stronger than one who cannot."

"Well then," she continued, "the highest good is proposed equally to good and bad men. Good men seek it by the natural

means of the virtues; evil men, however, try to achieve the
same goal by a variety of concupiscences, and that is surely
an unnatural way of seeking the good. Don't you agree?"

"I do, indeed. And I see clearly the consequence of your
line of reasoning. For it follows that the good are powerful
and the wicked are impotent."

"Your deduction is correct and indicates to your physician
an improving state of health and resistance. But since I see
that you are so quick to understand, I will condense my
demonstration. Consider how great is the weakness of vicious
men who are unable to achieve that goal toward which their
nature leads, even forces, them. What would happen if they were
deprived of this great and nearly irresistible natural tendency?
Think how grave is this impotence of wicked men. For the
goal which they are pursuing is not a trivial or frivolous
thing; they fail in the race for the very summit of all things;
they fail miserably to achieve even the things for which they
struggle night and day. And just here the powers of good
men are clearly seen. For, as you would consider an effective
walker one who could go on foot as far as it is possible to go,
so you must consider him to be most powerful who achieves
the goal of all human desires, the good beyond which there
is nothing. An obvious conclusion follows from this: the
wicked are wholly deprived of strength. For why do they
neglect virtue and pursue vice? Is it because they are ignorant
of the good? Well, what greater weakness is there than the
blindness of ignorance? Or do they know what they should
seek, but are driven astray by lust? If so, they are made weak
by intemperance and cannot overcome their vices. Or, do they
knowingly and willfully desert the good and turn to vice?
Anyone acting that way loses not only his strength but his
very being, since to forsake the common goal of all existence
is to forsake existence itself.

"Perhaps it may strike some as strange to say that evil men
do not exist, especially since they are so numerous; but it is
not so strange. For I do not deny that those who are evil are
evil; but I do deny that they *are,* in the pure and simple sense

of the term. For just as you may call a cadaver a dead man, but cannot call it simply a man, so I would concede that vicious men are evil, but I cannot say, in an absolute sense, that they exist. For a thing is which maintains its place in nature and acts in accord with its nature. Whatever fails to do this loses the existence which is proper to its nature. But you may argue that evil men are capable of action. I will not deny it, but such capability is the product of weakness, not of strength. For they can do evil acts which they could not have done if they had been able to remain capable of good. And that possibility of doing evil shows clearly that they can do nothing. For, if our earlier conclusion that evil is nothing still stands, it is clear that the wicked can do nothing since they can do only evil."

"That is evident," I agreed.

"And, so that you may understand what the nature of this power is, let me remind you what we have already proved that there is nothing more powerful than the Supreme Good."

"That is true."

"But," Philosophy went on, "the sovereign Good cannot do evil."

"Certainly not."

"And does anyone think that men can do all things?"

"No one in his right mind could think so."

"But men can do evil."

"Unfortunately, they can."

"Therefore, since He who can only do good can do all things, and those who can do evil cannot do all things, it is obvious that those who can do evil are less powerful. Moreover, we have already shown that every kind of power is included among the things which men desire, and that all objects of human desire are related to the good as the goal of their natures. But the ability to commit crime is not related to the good, and so it is not desirable. And, since every power should be desired, it follows that the power to do evil is not a power at all. From all this it is clear that good men have power, but evil men are weak. Likewise, the truth of Plato's doctrine is evident; only the wise can do what they want to do; the wicked can follow their desires, but they cannot accomplish what they want. For they do what they feel like doing, and they suppose that they will find among their pleasures the good they are really looking for. But they are bound to fail, since shameful behavior does not bring happiness.

POEM 2

"Those high and mighty kings you see sitting on high in glory, dressed in purple, surrounded by armed guards, can breathe cruel fury, threaten with fierce words. But if you strip off the coverings of vain honor from those proud men, you will see underneath the tight chains they wear. Lust rules their hearts with greedy poisons, rage whips them, vexing their minds to stormy wrath. Sometimes they are slaves to sorrow, sometimes to delusive hope. This is the picture of individual man with all his tyrant passions; enslaved by these evil powers, he cannot do what he wishes.

PROSE 3

The good are always rewarded and the wicked always punished.

"Do you see now the mire in which vice wallows, and the light in which probity shines? This shows clearly that the good are always rewarded and the wicked always punished. The aim or goal of an action may justly be said to be the reward of that action; as in a race, the prize a man competes for is said to be the reward. We have demonstrated that happiness is the good for which all things are done. Absolute good, therefore, is set up as a kind of common prize for all human activity. Now this prize is always achieved by good men, and further, no one who lacks the good may rightly be called a good man. Therefore, men of moral probity always achieve their reward. No matter how the wicked rave, the wise man never loses his prize; nor does it ever diminish.

"The wickedness of others does not deprive virtuous men of their glory. But if a man should find his happiness in a reward received from someone else, then either the one who gave it, or some other person, could take it away. But since a man's own probity confers this reward, he can lose the reward only by ceasing to be virtuous. Finally, since every reward is desired precisely because it is believed to be good, who can think that one who possesses good is without his reward?

"And what a reward it is, the greatest and best of all! For recall the corollary I showed you before [1] and make this inference: since the good is happiness, all good men are made happy by the very fact that they are good. And we have already shown that those who are happy are gods. Therefore, the reward of good men, which time cannot lessen, nor power diminish, nor the wickedness of any man tarnish, is to become gods.

"Since this is so, the wise man can be certain of the punishment of the wicked. For, since good and evil, reward and punishment, are opposites, the rewards of the good necessarily indicate the opposite—the punishment of the wicked. Therefore, just as virtue is the reward of virtuous men, so wickedness itself is the punishment of the wicked. Certainly, when a man is punished he knows that he suffers evil. And, if they think about their condition, can those who are not only tainted, but even infected by vice, the worst of all evils, consider themselves free from punishment? Consider the punishment which afflicts the evil as compared with the rewards of the good. You learned earlier that whatever is, is one, and that whatever is one, is good; it follows then that whatever is must also be good. And it follows from this that whatever loses its goodness ceases to be. Thus wicked men cease to be what they were; but the appearance of their human bodies, which they keep, shows that they once were men. To give oneself to evil, therefore, is to lose one's human nature. Just as virtue can raise a person above human nature, so vice lowers those whom

[1] See Book III, Prose 10.

it has seduced from the condition of men beneath human nature. For this reason, anyone whom you find transformed by vice cannot be counted a man.

"You will say that the man who is driven by avarice to seize what belongs to others is like a wolf; the restless, angry man who spends his life in quarrels you will compare to a dog. The treacherous conspirator who steals by fraud may be likened to a fox; the man who is ruled by intemperate anger is thought to have the soul of a lion. The fearful and timid man who trembles without reason is like a deer; the lazy, stupid fellow is like an ass. The volatile, inconstant man who continually changes direction is like a bird; the man who is sunk in foul lust is trapped in the pleasures of a filthy sow. In this way, anyone who abandons virtue ceases to be a man, since he cannot share in the divine nature, and instead becomes a beast.

Poem 3

"Eurus, the east wind, caught the sails of Ulysses' wandering ships and drove them to the island where lived the fair goddess Circe, daughter of the Sun. She mixed for her new guests a drink tainted by her magic, and by her skillful use of herbs she changed the sailors into different shapes. Some grew the faces of wild boars, others became African lions with sharp teeth and claws; some were turned into wolves, and when they tried to cry they howled; others wandered meekly about the house like Indian tigers.

"But, in spite of so many misfortunes, Mercury, the winged God of Arcady, had mercy on Ulysses and saved him from the poison of his hostess. Nevertheless, his sailors greedily drank the evil cups; they were changed into swine and turned from food to husks and acorns. No part of them remained unchanged—they lost both voice and body; only the mind remained to mourn the monstrous change they had suffered.

"But see how weak was the power of the goddess and her

impotent herbs. She had power over the bodies of men, but could not change their hearts. The strength of man is within, hidden in the remote tower of the heart. Poisons which can make him forget himself are more potent and deadly than Circe's because they corrupt the inner man. They do not harm the body, but they horribly wound the mind."

Prose 4

Philosophy argues that, in spite of appearances, the wicked are impotent and miserably unhappy.

When she had finished, I said, "I see that you are right in saying that; although vicious men keep the appearance of their human bodies, they are nevertheless changed into beasts as far as the character of their souls is concerned. Still, I wish that these cruel and wicked minds were not permitted to ruin good men."

"They are not permitted to do that, as I shall show you at the proper time. If, however, the power which they are thought to have were taken from them, their punishment would be greatly diminished. For, though this may seem incredible to some, the wicked are necessarily more unhappy when they have their way than they would be if they could not do what they wanted to do. If it is bad to desire evil, it is worse to be able to accomplish it; for if it were not accomplished, the disordered will would be ineffectual. So, when you see someone with the will and the power to commit crime actually commit it, you know that he is necessarily the victim of a threefold misfortune; for each of those three things—the will, the power, and the act itself—contains its own punishment."

"I grant that," I answered. "But I hope that they may quickly be relieved of this misfortune by losing their power to commit crime."

"They will lose it sooner than you may wish, perhaps, and sooner than they think. For nothing happens so slowly in the brief span of this life that the immortal spirit finds it long to wait for; the high hopes and well-laid plots of the wicked are often quickly and unexpectedly destroyed, and this does, indeed, limit their misery.

"If wickedness makes men miserable, the longer they are wicked the more wretched they must be. And I would consider most unhappy those who did not finally find an end to their wickedness in death. If, then, we have found out the truth about the misery of wickedness, it is clear that unhappiness which lasts forever must be infinite."

"That is a strange and difficult conclusion," I said, "but I recognize that it follows from that which I have already conceded to be true."

"You are right," Philosophy answered, "but anyone who finds it hard to accept a conclusion ought either to point out a false step in the argument or show that the series of propositions does not indicate a necessary conclusion. Otherwise he must grant the inference if he has granted the premises.

"What I am now about to say may seem equally surprising, yet it follows with equal certainty from my argument."

"What is it?" I asked.

"That the wicked are happier when they are punished than when they evade justice. I am not now suggesting the argument that might occur to anyone, that vicious men are corrected by punishment or led to reform by the fear of it, or that such punishment sets an example to others so that they will avoid involvement in crime. In addition to the possibility of correcting and the power of example, there is still another way in which the wicked who avoid punishment can be shown to be more unhappy than those who are punished."

"What is that?" I asked.

"We have shown, have we not, that the good are happy and the wicked unhappy?"

"Yes."

"If, then, an unhappy man achieves some good, is he not happier than the man whose unhappiness is complete and unmixed with the slightest good?"

"I should think so," I said.

"And, if the misery of the man who has no good at all is increased by additional evils, isn't he much unhappier than the man who is relieved by acquiring some good?"

"Yes, of course."

"Therefore, the wicked receive some good when they are punished, because the punishment itself is good inasmuch as it is just; conversely, when the wicked avoid punishment, they become more evil, because you have already admitted that such impunity is evil because it is unjust."

"I cannot deny that."

"Therefore, the wicked who unjustly escape punishment are more unhappy than those who are justly punished."

"I agree that this follows from what has already been proved. But," I asked, "do you leave no room for the punishment of souls after the death of the body?"

"I do, indeed," Philosophy answered, "and such punishments are severe. Some are imposed as bitter penalties, others as merciful purgation. But it is not now my intention to speak of these. So far I have tried to make you see that the power of evil men, which you find intolerable, does not exist, and that those same men, whom you think go unpunished, really never escape the penalties of their wickedness. Further, I have shown that their apparent impunity is short-lived, that the longer it goes on the unhappier they become, and that if it were eternal they would be absolutely wretched. Finally, I have proved that wicked men who unjustly escape punishment are more miserable than those who are justly punished. And it follows from this that when they seem to escape chastisement, they are in reality undergoing more severe punishment."

"When I consider your argument," I said, "I find that nothing could be more true. But, if we consider the ordinary judgment of men, who is likely to find these ideas credible, or who will even listen to them?"

"That is true," Philosophy answered, "because men cannot raise eyes accustomed to darkness to the light of clear truth. They are like those birds who can see at night but are blind in the daylight. For as long as they fix their attention on their own feelings, rather than on the true nature of things, they think that the license of passion and immunity from punishment bring happiness. But think of the sanctions of eternal law. If you conform your spirit to better things, you have no need of human approval and reward; you have placed yourself among the more excellent. But, if you turn to what is cheap and low, do not expect someone else to punish you; you will have lowered yourself to a condition of squalor. It is as if you were to look by turns at the sordid earth and at the heavens, compelled by the power of sight—and nothing else—to be now in the dirt, now among the stars. Just because thoughtless men do not understand this, should we lower ourselves to those whom we have shown to be like beasts? If a man who had completely lost his sight should forget that he had ever been able to see, and be quite unaware of any natural disability, would we too think that this blind man could see?

"Most thoughtless people will not even grant another equally strong argument to the effect that those who injure others are more unhappy than those whom they injure."

"I would like to hear your explanation of that."

"Would you deny that every wicked man deserves to be punished?"

"No."

"And is it absolutely clear that the wicked are unhappy?"

"Yes."

"Then you agree that those who deserve punishment are miserable."

"That follows," I agreed.

"Then, if you were the judge, whom would you punish: the one who did the injury, or the one who suffered it?"

"Without any hesitation I would satisfy the injured party by punishing the one who hurt him."

"Then you must be convinced that the one who does evil is more miserable than the one to whom evil is done."

"That follows."

"From this, then, and for other reasons based on the principle that wickedness by its very nature makes men miserable, we see that an injury done to another causes unhappiness in the doer rather than in the recipient. But at present, lawyers take the opposite tack. They try to arouse sympathy in the judges for those who have suffered grave injury, when those who have harmed them are much more deserving of pity. Such criminals ought to be brought to justice by kind and compassionate accusers, as sick men are taken to the doctor, so that their disease of guilt might be cured by punishment. In this way, defense attorneys could be dispensed with, or, if they wanted to help their clients, they would become accusers. And, if the wicked themselves could somehow see the virtue they had abandoned, and could be convinced that they could free themselves from the stain of vice and acquire virtue by undergoing punishment, they would ignore the pain, dismiss their lawyers, and give themselves up entirely to their accusers and judges.

"In this way, wise men could abolish hatred; for no one but a fool would hate good men, and hating evil men would make no sense. Viciousness is a kind of disease of the soul, like illness in the body. And if sickness of the body is not something we hate, but rather regard with sympathy, we have much more reason to pity those whose minds are afflicted with wickedness, a thing worse than any sickness.

POEM 4

"Why do you whip yourselves to frenzy, and ever seek your fate by self-destruction? If you look for death, she stands nearby of her own accord; she does not restrain her swift horses. Those whom snakes, lions, tigers, bears, and boars are poised to kill raise their weapons against each other. Do men raise unjust quarrels and fierce wars because their lands and customs are different? Is this why they seek death from each other? Surely this is not just cause for such cruelty. If you would give every man what he deserves, then love the good and pity those who are evil."

PROSE 5

Boethius continues to wonder why an all-powerful God seems sometimes to reward the wicked with happiness and to afflict the good with sorrow.

Then I said, "I understand that happiness and misery come to good and wicked men according to their merits. Still, I find that there is a mixture of some good and some evil in every man's fortune, as that term is popularly understood. Surely no wise man wants to live in exile, poverty, and ignominy; he would rather live prosperously in his own country, and enjoy riches, honors, and the exercise of power. The operation of wisdom is manifested more effectively and recognized more clearly when the happiness of those who govern is shared by the people; and this is especially true when imprisonment and other consequences of legal punishment are imposed on the criminals for whom they were intended. Therefore I am amazed and shocked to find this ideal turned upside down, so that punishments designed for the wicked are imposed on good men, and the rewards of virtue are seized by the wicked. I wish you would tell me how such unjust confusion can possibly be explained. For I would be less surprised if I could believe that all things happened as the result of accidental chance. But my belief in God and his governing power increases my amazement. Since He often gives joy to the good and bitterness to the wicked, but on the other hand often reverses this dispensation, how can all this be distinguished from accidental chance unless we understand the cause of it?"

"It is no wonder," Philosophy answered, "that a situation should seem random and confused when its principle of order is not understood. But, although you do not know why things are as they are, still you cannot doubt that in a world ruled by a good Governor all things do happen justly.

POEM 5

"The man who does not know why the stars of Arcturus turn near the highest pole, nor why slow Boötes drives his chariot to dip his flames into the sea, yet rises again so quickly, must be amazed by the laws of celestial bodies. When the horns of the full moon grow pale, dimmed by the darkness of night, and the stars which Phoebe had obscured with her shining face are now uncovered, popular error excites the people and they beat brazen cymbals with rapid blows.[2]

"No one wonders why the storms of Corus [3] beat the shore with pounding waves, nor why the frozen drifts of snow are melted by the hot rays of the sun. The causes of such natural phenomena are quickly understood; but those others are obscure and disturb the mind. All sudden and rare events bewilder the unstable and the uninformed. But if the cloudy error of ignorance is swept away, such things will seem strange no longer."

PROSE 6

Philosophy discourses on Providence and Fate. She shows that what may seem unjust confusion in the affairs of men is directed by Providence toward the good.

"That is true," I said. "But, since you can reveal the hidden cause of things and throw light on reasons that are veiled in darkness, I beg you to tell me what you know about this apparent injustice which I find so inexplicable and troublesome."

Then she smiled a little and said, "You are asking about the

2 Boethius refers to the ancient superstition that an eclipse of the moon threatened loss of it, and that the noise of cymbals could bring it back. See Juvenal, *Satires* 6. 442ff.

3 Corus, a river of Arabia which flows into the Red Sea.

greatest of all mysteries, one which can hardly be fully explained. This problem is such that when one doubt is cleared up many more arise like the heads of the Hydra, and continue to spring up unless they are checked by the most active fire of the mind. Among the many questions raised by this problem are these: the simplicity of Providence, the course of Fate, unforeseeable chance, divine knowledge and predestination, and free will. You yourself know how difficult these questions are, but since it is part of your medicine to know these things, I shall try to say something about them even though our time is short. But you will have to do without the pleasure of verse for a while as I put together the pattern of my argument."

"As you wish," I said.

Then, as though she were making a new beginning, Philosophy explained: "The generation of all things, and the whole course of mutable natures and of whatever is in any way subject to change, take their causes, order, and forms from the unchanging mind of God. This divine mind established the manifold rules by which all things are governed while it remained in the secure castle of its own simplicity. When this government is regarded as belonging to the purity of the divine mind, it is called Providence; but when it is considered with reference to the things which it moves and governs, it has from very early times been called Fate. It is easy to see that Providence and Fate are different if we consider the power of each. Providence is the divine reason itself which belongs to the most high ruler of all things and which governs all things; Fate, however, belongs to all mutable things and is the disposition by which Providence joins all things in their own order. For Providence embraces all things equally, however diverse they are, however infinite. Fate, on the other hand, sets particular things in motion once they have been given their own forms, places, and times. Thus Providence is the unfolding of temporal events as this is present to the vision of the divine mind; but this same unfolding of events as it is worked out in time is called Fate. Although the two are different things, one depends upon the other, for the process of Fate

derives from the simplicity of Providence. Just as the crafts-
man conceives in his mind the form of the thing he intends
to make, and then sets about making it by producing in suc-
cessive temporal acts that which was simply present in his
mind, so God by his Providence simply and unchangeably disposes all things that are to be done, even though the things
themselves are worked out by Fate in many ways and in the
process of time.

"Therefore, whether Fate is carried out by divine spirits in
the service of Providence, or by a soul, or by the whole activity of nature, by the heavenly motions of the stars, by
angelic virtue or diabolical cleverness, or by some or all of these
agents, one thing is certain: Providence is the immovable and
simple form of all things which come into being, while Fate
is the moving connection and temporal order of all things
which the divine simplicity has decided to bring into being. It
follows then, that everything which is subject to Fate is also
subject to Providence, and that Fate itself is also subject to
Providence.

"Some things, however, which are subject to Providence
are above the force of Fate and ungoverned by it. Consider the
example of a number of spheres in orbit around the same
central point: the innermost moves toward the simplicity of
the center and becomes a kind of hinge about which the outer
spheres circle; whereas the outermost, whirling in a wider
orbit, tends to increase its orbit in space the farther it moves
from the indivisible midpoint of the center. If, however, it is
connected to the center, it is confined by the simplicity of the
center and no longer tends to stray into space. In like manner,
whatever strays farthest from the divine mind is most en-
tangled in the nets of Fate; conversely, the freer a thing is
from Fate, the nearer it approaches the center of all things.
And if it adheres firmly to the divine mind, it is free from motion and overcomes the necessity of Fate. Therefore, the changing course of Fate is to the simple stability of Providence as
reasoning is to intellect, as that which is generated is to that
which *is*, as time is to eternity, as a circle to its center. Fate

moves the heavens and the stars, governs the elements in their mixture, and transforms them by mutual change; it renews all things that are born and die by the reproduction of similar off-spring and seeds. This same power binds the actions and for-tunes of men in an unbreakable chain of causes and, since these causes have their origins in an unchangeable Providence, they too must necessarily be unchangeable. In this way things are governed perfectly when the simplicity residing in the di-vine mind produces an unchangeable order of causes. This order, by its own unchanging nature, controls mutable things which otherwise would be disordered and confused.

"Therefore, even though things may seem confused and dis-cordant to you, because you cannot discern the order that governs them, nevertheless everything is governed by its own proper order directing all things toward the good. Nothing is done for the sake of evil, even by wicked men who, as I have proved, are actually seeking the good when they are perverted by wretched error, since the order which flows from the center of the highest good does not turn anyone aside from his original course.

"But, you ask, what worse confusion can there be than for the good to enjoy prosperity and suffer adversity, and for the wicked also to get both what they want and what they cannot bear? But is human judgment so infallible that those who are thought to be good and evil are necessarily what they seem to be? If so, why are men's judgments so often in conflict, so that the same men are thought by some to deserve reward and by others punishment? And, even granting that someone can dis-tinguish between good and evil persons, can he, like the doc-tor examining the body of his patient, look into the inner temper of the soul? The problems of such judgments are similar: for it is a mystery to the layman why some healthy persons find sweet foods agreeable, others sour foods, and why some sick persons are helped by gentle treatment, others by harsh medicines. The physician, however, does not find such things at all strange because he understands the nature of sickness and health. Now, what is the health of souls but virtue, and what is their sickness but vice? And who, indeed, is the preserver of the good and the corrector of the wicked but God, the governor and physician of men's minds, who looks into the great mirror of his providence and, knowing what is best for each one, causes it to happen? Here, then, is the great miracle of the order of Fate: divine wisdom does what the ignorant cannot understand.

"I shall limit my discussion of the divine judgment to a few things which human reason can comprehend. The man whom you think most just and honorable may seem quite otherwise to the Providence which knows all things. Thus my disciple Lucan observed that, although Cato favored the side of those who were conquered, the gods favored the conquerors.[4] Therefore, when you see something happen here contrary to your ideas of what is right, it is your opinion and expectation which is confused, while the order in things themselves is right. Take, for example, the man so fortunate as to seem approved by both God and men; he may actually be so weak in character that if he were to suffer adversity he would forsake virtue on the grounds that it seemed not to bring him good fortune. Therefore God in his wise dispensation spares the man whom adversity might ruin, so that he may not suffer who cannot stand suffering. Another man who is perfect in all virtues, holy, and dear to God, may be spared even bodily sickness because Providence judges it wrong for him to be touched by any adversity at all. As one who is better than I put it: 'the body of the holy man is made of pure ether.'[5] It often happens that supreme rule is given to good men so that infectious evil may be held in check. To others, Providence gives a mixture of prosperity and adversity according to the disposi-

---

[4] Lucan, *Pharsalia* I. 128. In this work, Lucan, a Roman poet of the first century, deals with the Civil War in which Caesar was finally victorious. Cato the Younger, Roman Stoic philosopher, committed suicide rather than survive Caesar's victory at Thapsus in 46 B.C. because he felt that the Republic was destroyed.

[5] The Greek hexameter quoted here is from an unknown source. "Ether," Greek αἰθέρες, suggests those powers or virtues which belong to the heavens between God and earth.

tion of their souls: she gives trouble to some whom too much
luxury might spoil; others she tests with hardships in order
to strengthen their virtues by the exercise of patience. Some
people fear to undertake burdens they could easily bear, while
others treat too lightly those they are unable to handle; both
types are led on by Providence to find themselves by trials.
Some have earned worldly fame at the price of glorious death;
others, by not breaking under torture, have proved to the
world that virtue cannot be conquered by evil. No one can
doubt that such trials are good and just and beneficial to
those who suffer them.

"Moreover, the lot of the wicked, which is sometimes painful and sometimes easy, comes from the same source and for
the same reasons. No one wonders at the troubles they
undergo, since everyone thinks that is just what they deserve.
Such punishment both deters others from crime and prompts
those who suffer it to reform. On the other hand, the prosperity of the wicked is a powerful argument for the good, because they see how they ought to evaluate the kind of good
fortune which the wicked so often enjoy. Still another good
purpose may be served by the prosperity of the wicked man:
if his nature is so reckless and violent that poverty might
drive him to crime, Providence may cure this morbid tendency
by making him wealthy. When such a man recognizes his
viciousness and contrasts his guilt with his fortune, he may
perhaps become alarmed at the painful consequences of losing what he enjoys so much. He will then change his ways
and behave himself as long as he fears the loss of his wealth.
Some who have achieved prosperity unworthily have been
driven by it to well deserved ruin. Some have been given the
right to punish so that the good might be tested and the evil
punished. For just as there is no agreement between the just
and the unjust, so the unjust themselves cannot get along together. And why not, since such men are at odds with themselves and their vicious consciences, and often regret their own
foolish actions. From this condition the highest Providence
often brings about the miracle by which the wicked make

other wicked men good. For, when they find themselves unjustly persecuted by vicious men, they burn with hatred
against them and return to the practice of virtue because they
cannot bear to be like those whom they hate. Only to divine
power are evil things good, when it uses them so as to draw
good effects from them. All things are part of a certain order,
so that when something moves away from its assigned place,
it falls into a new order of things. Nothing in the realm of
Providence is left to chance.

" 'But it is hard for me to recount all this as if I were a
God,' [6] for it is not fitting for men to understand intellectually
or to explain verbally all the dispositions of the divine work.
It is enough to have understood only that God, the Creator of
all things in nature, also governs all things, directing them to
good. And, since He carefully preserves everything which He
made in his own likeness, He excludes by fatal necessity all
evil from the bounds of his state. Therefore, if you fix your
attention on Providence as the governor of all things, you will
find that the evil which is thought to abound in the world is
really nonexistent. But I see that you are weary from listening
so long to this extended and difficult discourse and want to be
refreshed by poetry. Listen then, and gather your strength for
what is yet to be explained.

POEM 6

"If you wish to discern the laws of the high and mighty
God, the high thunderer, with an unclouded mind, look
up to the roof of highest heaven. There the stars, united by
just agreement, keep the ancient peace. The sun, driven by
red fire, does not impede the cold circle of Phoebe. Nor
does the Great Bear driving its course at the world's top
hide itself in the western ocean; it never wants to drown
its flames in the sea, though it sees other stars plunge beneath the waves. The faithful Hesperus announces the ap-

[6] Homer, *Iliad* XII. 176.

proach of night at the assigned time; then, as Lucifer, it brings back the warming day.[7]

"Thus mutual love governs their eternal movement and the war of discord is excluded from the bounds of heaven. Concord rules the elements with fair restraint: moist things yield place to dry, cold and hot combine in friendship; flickering fire rises on high, and gross earth sinks down. Impelled by the same causes, the flowering year breathes out its odors in warm spring; hot summer dries the grain and autumn comes in burdened with fruit; then falling rain brings in wet winter.

"This ordered change nourishes and sustains all that lives on earth; then snatches away and buries all that was born, hiding it in final death. Meanwhile, the Creator sits on high, governing and guiding the course of things. King and lord, source and origin, law and wise judge of right. All things which He placed in motion, He draws back and holds in check; He makes firm whatever tends to stray. If He did not recall them to their true paths and set them again on their circling courses, all things that the stable order now contains would be wrenched from their source and perish.

"This is the common bond of love by which all things seek to be held to the goal of good. Only thus can things endure: drawn by love they turn again to the Cause which gave them being.

Prose 7

Philosophy, at the request of Boethius, restates in popular form her thesis that all fortune is good.

"And now," said Philosophy, "do you understand the implications of what I have told you?"

"What do you mean?" I asked.

"That all fortune is good."

---

[7] Both these stars refer to the planet Venus. See p. 15, note 20.

"But how can that be?" I said.

"Look here," Philosophy answered. "Since all fortune, whether sweet or bitter, has as its purpose the reward or trial of good men or the correction and punishment of the wicked, it must be good because it is clearly either just or useful."

"Your reasoning is true," I said, "and your explanation is sound, especially when I consider what you have taught me about Providence and Fate. But if you don't mind, we ought to put this among the doctrines which you not long ago called surprising."

"Why so?" Philosophy asked.

"Because people ordinarily hold that some men suffer bad fortune."

"You mean that you want to accommodate our discourse to the common speech so that we will not move too far from ordinary human ways?"

"Yes, if you don't mind."

"Well, then, do you agree that whatever is profitable is good?"

"Yes."

"And that whatever tests or corrects is profitable?"

"Yes."

"And therefore good?"

"Yes."

"This, then, is the situation of the virtuous who struggle courageously against misfortune, or of those who are trying to reform and become virtuous."

"That is quite true," I said.

"And what about the prosperity which is given to good men as a reward; do ordinary people think that bad?"

"No. They rightly consider it to be very good."

"Well then, what about the adversity which restrains the wicked by punishing them justly?"

"Quite the contrary," I answered. "They consider that the worst fate that can be imagined."

"Then notice that by following the popular opinion of the people we have arrived at a most surprising conclusion."

"How so?" I asked.

"Our argument so far has proved that the fortune of the virtuous, or of those who are advancing toward virtue, is good, whatever it may be; but the fortune of those who continue in wickedness is bad."

"That is true," I said, "but no one would dare say so."

"A wise man ought not to regret his struggles with fortune any more than a brave soldier should be intimidated by the noise of battle; for difficulty is the natural lot of each. For the soldier it is the source of increasing glory; for the wise man it is the means of confirming his wisdom. Indeed, virtue gets its name from that virile strength which is not overcome by adversity. And you, who are advancing in virtue, should not expect to be weakened by ease or softened by pleasure. You fight manfully against any fortune, neither despairing in the face of misfortune nor becoming corrupt in the enjoyment of prosperity. Hold fast to the middle ground with courage. Those who fall short or go too far are scornful of happiness and are deprived of the reward of labor. You can make of your fortune what you will; for any fortune which seems difficult either tests virtue or corrects and punishes vice.

POEM 7

"Agamemnon, the avenging son of Atreus, waged war for ten years until, by devastating Troy, he purged the dishonor done his brother's marriage. When he wished to fill the sails of the Greek fleet, and bring back the winds by a bloody sacrifice, he put off the role of father and, as a sorrowing priest, cut the throat of his daughter.[8]

"Ulysses mourned his lost comrades whom fierce Poly-

---

[8] Agamemnon's brother, Menelaus, was married to Helen, who was carried off by Paris of Troy. Agamemnon was commander-in-chief of the Greek forces to avenge the rape of Helen. When his fleet was detained by contrary winds at Aulis he sacrificed his daughter Iphigenia, to appease the wrath of Diana. Cf. Seneca, *Agamemnon*.

phemus, lying in his dark cave, had devoured into his vast belly; but the monster, driven mad by his blinded eye, repaid those former tears with joy.[9]

"Hercules is famous for his hard labors. He tamed the proud Centaurs; won' the spoils of the fierce Nemean lion; shot down the Stymphalian birds with his sure arrows; stole the golden apples from the watchful dragon; and shackled Cerberus with a triple chain. He conquered Diomede and fed the savage mares their cruel master's flesh. He burned the Hydra's poison heads, shamed the river Achelous by breaking his horns and made him bury his face in his banks. He killed Antaeus on the Libyan beach, and slew Cacus to slake the wrath of Evander. The boar marked with foam those shoulders which were to bear the weight of heaven. For his last labor he bore heaven on his strong neck, and for this he won again the prize of heaven.[10]

"Go now, strong men! Follow the high road of great example. Why slack off and turn your backs? When you overcome the earth, the stars will be yours."

[9] Ulysses joined in the battle against Troy. On his journey home, he suffered many hardships including an encounter with Polyphemus, King of the giant, one-eyed Cyclopes, in Sicily. Polyphemus devoured five of Ulysses' men; but Ulysses himself escaped by intoxicating the Cyclops and blinding his eye.

[10] Hercules was for twelve years subject to Eurystheus, King of Mycenae, who commanded him to undertake twelve famous labors. For completing these, Hercules achieved divinity. Many other exploits were attributed to him in antiquity and the Middle Ages. See Seneca, *Hercules Furens*.

BOOK V

PROSE 1

Philosophy discusses the question of chance.

When Philosophy had finished her song and was about to turn to the discussion of other matters, I interrupted saying, "Your exhortation is a worthy one and your authority is great, but I know from experience that you are right in saying that the question of Providence involves many other problems. I should like to know whether there is any such thing as chance, and, if so, what it may be."

"I have been trying, as quickly as possible, to carry out my promise to show you the way back to your true country. These other questions are somewhat beside the main point of my argument, even though they are quite important in themselves. I shouldn't want you to become so wearied by side trips that you would not be able to complete the main journey."

"Please do not worry about that," I said. "For it would comfort me to understand the things in which I take the greatest pleasure. When every part of your argument is convincingly established, none of its implications will cause any doubt."

"I will do as you ask," she replied, and took up her explanation again.

"If chance is defined as an event produced by random motion and without any sequence of causes, then I say that there is no such thing as chance; apart from its use in the present context, I consider it an empty word. For what room can there be for random events since God keeps all things in order? The commonplace that nothing can come from nothing is true; and the old philosophers never denied it, though they did not apply it to the effective cause of things but only to the material subject as a kind of foundation of all their reasoning about nature. But if anything should happen without cause, it would

101

seem to come from nothing. And if this cannot be, chance as we defined it a moment ago is impossible."

"Then is there nothing which can rightly be called chance?" I asked. "Does nothing happen fortuitously? Or is there something to which those words refer, even if it is not rightly understood by ordinary people?"

"My true follower, Aristotle, gave a brief and sound definition of chance in his *Physics*." [1]

"What did he say?" I asked.

"Whenever anything is done for one reason, but something other than what was intended happens on account of other reasons, it is called chance. For example, when a man digs the earth with the intention of cultivating it, and finds a treasure of buried gold, this is thought to happen by chance. But it does not come from nothing since the event has its own causes whose unforeseen and unexpected concurrence seems to have produced an effect by chance. For, if the farmer had not dug the ground, and if someone had not buried his gold in that spot, the treasure would not have been found. These are the causes of the fortunate accident which is brought about by the coincidence of causes and not by the intention of the one performing the action. For neither the man who buried the gold, nor the man who was cultivating the field, intended that the money should be found; but, as I said, it happened coincidentally that the farmer dug where the other had buried the money.

"Therefore, we can define chance as an unexpected event brought about by a concurrence of causes which had other purposes in view. These causes come together because of that order which proceeds from inevitable connection of things, the order which flows from the source which is Providence and which disposes all things, each in its proper time and place.

[1] *Physics* II. 4-5; cf. *Metaphysics* IV. 30.

POEM 1

"The Tigris and Euphrates flow from a single source in the Achaemenian rocks, where the Parthian warrior turns in his flight to shoot his arrows into the pursuing enemy, but they quickly flow apart in separate streams.[2] If they should join their waters again in one channel, all that each stream carries would come together; the boats that sail on each, the floating trees torn up by floods, and the waters too would mingle by chance. But steep channels and the downward flow of the current govern these seemingly random events. Chance, too, which seems to rush along with slack reins, is bridled and governed by law."

PROSE 2

Philosophy argues that rational natures must necessarily have free will.

"I have listened carefully and agree that chance is as you say. But, within this series of connected causes, does our will have any freedom, or are the motions of human souls also bound by the fatal chain?"

"There is free will," Philosophy answered, "and no rational nature can exist which does not have it. For any being, which by its nature has the use of reason, must also have the power of judgment by which it can make decisions and, by its own resources, distinguish between things which should be desired and things which should be avoided. Now everyone seeks that which he judges to be desirable, but rejects whatever he thinks should be avoided. Therefore, in rational creatures there is also freedom of desiring and shunning.

"But I do not say that this freedom is the same in all beings.

2 The Achaemenian rocks are in Armenia where both the Tigris and Euphrates originate. The Parthian warriors were famous for their skill in shooting arrows while retreating at full speed.

In supreme and divine substances there is clear judgment, un-corrupted will, and effective power to obtain what they desire. Human souls, however, are more free while they are engaged in contemplation of the divine mind, and less free when they are joined to bodies, and still less free when they are bound by earthly fetters. They are in utter slavery when they lose posses-sion of their reason and give themselves wholly to vice. For when they turn away their eyes from the light of supreme truth to mean and dark things, they are blinded by a cloud of ignorance and obsessed by vicious passions. By yielding and consenting to these passions, they worsen the slavery to which they have brought themselves and are, as it were, the captives of their own freedom. Nevertheless, God, who beholds all things from eternity, foresees all these things in his providence and disposes each according to its predestined merits.

POEM 2

" 'He sees all things and hears all things.' [3] Sweet-voiced Homer sings of the clear light of bright Phoebus; but the sun's weak rays cannot pierce the bowels of the earth nor the depths of the sea. It is not so with the Creator of this great sphere. No mass of earth, no dark and clouded night can re-sist his vision which looks down on all things. He sees at once, in a single glance, all things that are, or were, or are to come. Since He is sole observer of all things, you may call Him the true Sun."

PROSE 3

Boethius contends that divine foreknowledge and freedom of the human will are incompatible.

"Now I am confused by an even greater difficulty," I said.

"What is it?" Philosophy answered, "though I think I know what is bothering you."

"There seems to be a hopeless conflict between divine fore-

[3] *Iliad* III. 277; *Odyssey* XI. 109, and XII. 323.

knowledge of all things and freedom of the human will. For if God sees everything in advance and cannot be deceived in any way, whatever his Providence foresees will happen, must happen. Therefore, if God foreknows eternally not only all the acts of men, but also their plans and wishes, there cannot be freedom of will; for nothing whatever can be done or even desired without its being known beforehand by the infallible Providence of God. If things could somehow be accomplished in some way other than that which God foresaw, his foreknowledge of the future would no longer be certain. Indeed, it would be merely uncertain opinion, and it would be wrong to think that of God.

"I cannot agree with the argument by which some people believe that they can solve this problem. They say that things do not happen because Providence foresees that they will happen, but, on the contrary, that Providence foresees what is to come because it will happen, and in this way they find the necessity to be in things, not in Providence. For, they say, it is not necessary that things should happen because they are foreseen, but only that things which will happen be foreseen—as though the problem were whether divine Providence is the cause of the necessity of future events, or the necessity of future events is the cause of divine Providence. But our concern is to prove that the fulfillment of things which God has foreseen is necessary, whatever the order of causes, even if the divine foreknowledge does not seem to make the occurrence of future events necessary. For example, if a man sits down, the opinion that he is sitting must be true; and conversely, if the opinion that someone is sitting be true, then that person must necessarily be sitting. Therefore, there is necessity in both cases: the man must be sitting and the opinion must be true. But the man is not sitting because the opinion is true; the opinion is true because the sitting came before the opinion about it. Therefore, even though the cause of truth came from one side, necessity is common to both.

"A similar line of reasoning applies to divine foreknowledge and future events. For even though the events are foreseen because they will happen, they do not happen because they are foreseen. Nevertheless, it is necessary either that things which are going to happen be foreseen by God, or that what God foresees will in fact happen; and either way the freedom of the human will is destroyed. But of course it is preposterous to say that the outcome of temporal things is the cause of eternal foreknowledge. Yet to suppose that God foresees future events because they are going to happen is the same as supposing that things which happened long ago are the cause of divine Providence. Furthermore, just as when I know that a thing is, that thing must necessarily be; so when I know that something will happen, it is necessary that it happen. It follows, then, that the outcome of something known in advance must necessarily take place.

"Finally, if anyone thinks that a thing is other than it actually is, he does not have knowledge but merely a fallible opinion, and that is quite different from the truth of knowledge. So, if the outcome of some future event is either uncertain or unnecessary, no one can know in advance whether or not it will happen. For just as true knowledge is not tainted by falsity, so that which is known by it cannot be otherwise than as it is known. And that is the reason why knowledge never deceives; things must necessarily be as true knowledge knows them to be. If this is so, how does God foreknow future possibilities whose existence is uncertain? If He thinks that things will inevitably happen which possibly will not happen, He is deceived. But it is wrong to say that, or even to think it. And if He merely knows that they may or may not happen, that is, if He knows only their contingent possibilities, what is such knowledge worth, since it does not know with certainty? Such knowledge is no better than that expressed by the ridiculous prophecy of Tiresias: 'Whatever I say will either be or not be.' [4] Divine Providence would be no better than human opinion if God judges as men do and knows only that uncertain events are doubtful. But if nothing can be uncertain to Him who is the most certain source of all things, the outcome is certain of all things which He knows with certainty shall be.

[4] Horace, *Satires* II. 5. 59.

"Therefore, there can be no freedom in human decisions and actions, since the divine mind, foreseeing everything without possibility of error, determines and forces the outcome of everything that is to happen. Once this is granted, it is clear that the structure of all human affairs must collapse. For it is pointless to assign rewards and punishment to the good and wicked since neither are deserved if the actions of men are not free and voluntary. Punishment of the wicked and recognition of the good, which are now considered just, will seem quite unjust since neither the good nor the wicked are governed by their own will but are forced by the inevitability of predetermination. Vice and virtue will be without meaning, and in their place there will be utter confusion about what is deserved. Finally, and this is the most blasphemous thought of all, it follows that the Author of all good must be made responsible for all human vice since the entire order of human events depends on Providence and nothing on man's intention.

"There is no use in hoping or praying for anything, for what is the point in hope or prayer when everything that man desires is determined by unalterable process? Thus man's only bonds with God, hope and prayer, are destroyed. We believe that our just humility may earn the priceless reward of divine grace, for this is the only way in which men seem able to communicate with God; we are joined to that inaccessible light by supplication before receiving what we ask. But if we hold that all future events are governed by necessity, and therefore that prayer has no value, what will be left to unite us to the sovereign Lord of all things? And so mankind must, as you said earlier, be cut off from its source and dwindle into nothing.[5]

POEM 3

"What cause of discord breaks the ties which ought to bind this union of things? What God has set such conflict between these two truths? Separately each is certain, but put together they cannot be reconciled. Is there no discord be-

5 See Book IV, Poem 6.

tween them? Can they exist side by side and be equally true?

"The human mind, overcome by the body's blindness, cannot discern by its dim light the delicate connections between things. But why does the mind burn with such desire to discover the hidden aspects of truth? Does it know what it is so eager to know? Then why does it go on laboriously trying to discover what it already knows? And if it does not know, why does it blindly continue the search? For who would want something of which he is unaware, or run after something he does not know? How can such a thing be found, or, if found, how would it be recognized by someone ignorant of its form?

"When the human mind knew the mind of God, did it know the whole and all its parts? Now the mind is shrouded in the clouds of the body, but it has not wholly forgotten itself; and, although it has lost its grasp of particulars, it still holds fast to the general truth. Therefore, whoever seeks the truth knows something: he is neither completely informed nor completely ignorant. He works with what he remembers of the highest truth, using what he saw on high in order to fill in the forgotten parts."

PROSE 4

Philosophy begins her argument that divine Providence does not preclude freedom of the will by stressing the difference between divine and human knowledge.

"This is an old difficulty about Providence," Philosophy answered. "It was raised by Cicero in his book on divination,[6] and has for a long time been a subject of your own investigation, but so far none of you has treated it with enough care and conviction. The cause of the obscurity which still surrounds the problem is that the process of human reason cannot comprehend the simplicity of divine foreknowledge. If in any way we could understand that, no further doubt would re-

6 *De divinatione* II. 8ff.

main. I shall try to make this clear after I have explained the
things which trouble you.

"First, let me ask why you regard as inconclusive the reasoning of those who think that foreknowledge is no hindrance to
free will because it is not the cause of the necessity of future
things. For do you have any argument for the necessity of
future events other than the principle that things which are
known beforehand must happen? If, as you have just now conceded, foreknowledge does not impose necessity on future
events, why must the voluntary outcome of things be bound to
predetermined results? For the sake of argument, so that you
may consider what follows from it, let us suppose that there is
no foreknowledge. Then would the things which are done by
free will be bound by necessity in this respect?"

"Not at all."

"Then, let us suppose that foreknowledge exists but imposes
no necessity on things. The same independence and absolute
freedom of will would remain.

"But you will say that even though foreknowledge does not
impose necessity on future events, it is still a sign that they will
necessarily happen. It must follow then that even if there were
no foreknowledge the outcome of these future things would be
necessary. For signs only show what is, they do not cause the
things they point to. Therefore we must first prove that nothing happens other than by necessity, in order to demonstrate
that foreknowledge is a sign of this necessity. Otherwise, if
there is no necessity, then foreknowledge cannot be a sign of
something that does not exist. Moreover, it is clear that firmly
based proof does not rest on signs and extrinsic arguments but
is deduced from suitable and necessary causes. But how can it
be that things which are foreseen should not happen? We do
not suppose that things will not happen, if Providence has
foreknowledge that they will; rather we judge that, although
they will happen, they have nothing in their natures which
makes it necessary that they should happen. For we see many
things in the process of happening before our eyes, just as the
chariot driver sees the results of his actions as he quides his

chariot; and this is true in many of our activities. Do you think that such things are compelled by necessity to happen as they do?"

"No. For the results of art would be vain if they were all brought about by compulsion."

"Then, since they come into being without necessity, these same things were not determined by necessity before they actually happened. Therefore, there are some things destined to happen in the future whose outcome is free of any necessity. For everyone, I think, would say that things which are now happening were going to happen before they actually came to pass. Thus, these things happen without necessity even though they were known in advance. For just as knowledge of things happening now does not imply necessity in their outcomes, so foreknowledge of future things imposes no necessity on their outcomes in the future.

"But, you will say, the point at issue is whether there can be any foreknowledge of things whose outcomes are not necessary. For these things seem opposed to each other, and you think that if things can be foreseen they must necessarily happen, and that if the necessity is absent they cannot be foreseen, and that nothing can be fully known unless it is certain. If uncertain things are foreseen as certain, that is the weakness of opinion, not the truth of knowledge. You believe that to judge that a thing is other than it is departs from the integrity of knowledge. Now the cause of this error lies in your assumption that whatever is known, is known only by the force and nature of the things which are known; but the opposite is true. Everything which is known is known not according to its own power but rather according to the capacity of the knower.

"Let me illustrate with a brief example: the roundness of a body is known in one way by the sense of touch and in another by the sight. The sight, remaining at a distance, takes in the whole body at once by its reflected rays; but the touch makes direct contact with the sphere and comprehends it piecemeal by moving around its surface. A man himself is comprehended in different ways by the senses, imagination, reason, and intel-

ligence. The senses grasp the figure of the thing as it is constituted in matter; the imagination, however, grasps the figure
alone without the matter. Reason, on the other hand, goes beyond this and investigates by universal consideration the species
itself which is in particular things. The vision of intelligence is
higher yet, and it goes beyond the bounds of the universe and
sees with the clear eye of the mind the pure form itself.

"In all this we chiefly observe that the higher power of
knowing includes the lower, but the lower can in no way rise
to the higher. For the senses achieve nothing beyond the material, the imagination cannot grasp universal species, reason
cannot know simple forms; but the intelligence, as though
looking down from on high, conceives the underlying forms
and distinguishes among them all, but in the same way in
which it comprehends the form itself which cannot be known
to any other power. The intelligence knows the objects of the
lower kinds of knowledge: the universals of the reason, the
figures of the imagination, the matter of the senses, but not by
using reason, or imagination, or senses. With a single glance of
the mind it formally, as it were, sees all things. Similarly,
when reason knows a universal nature, it comprehends all the
objects of imagination and the senses without using either. For
reason defines the general nature of her conception as follows:
man is a biped, rational animal. This is a universal idea, but
no one ignores the fact that man is also an imaginable and
sensible object which reason knows by rational conception
rather than by the imagination and senses. Similarly, although
the imagination begins by seeing and forming figures with the
senses, nevertheless it can, without the aid of the senses, behold sensible objects by an imaginative rather than a sensory
mode of knowing.

"Do you see, then, how all these use their own power in
knowing rather than the powers of the objects which are
known? And this is proper, for since all judgment is in the
act of the one judging, it is necessary that everyone should
accomplish his own action by his own power, not by the power
of something other than himself.

POEM 4

"Long ago the philosophers of the Porch at Athens,[7] old men who saw things dimly, believed that sense impressions and images were impressed on the mind by external objects, just as then they used to mark letters on a blank page of wax with their quick pens. But, if the active mind can discover nothing by its own powers, and merely remains passively subject to the impressions of external bodies, like a mirror reflecting the empty shapes of other things, where does that power come from which dwells in souls and sees all things? What is that power which perceives individual things and, by knowing them, can distinguish among them? What is the power which puts together again the parts it has separated and, pursuing its due course, lifts its gaze to the highest things, then descends again to the lowest, then returns to itself to refute false ideas with truth?

"This is a more effective, and a much more powerful cause than any which merely receives impressions from material things. Still, the sense impression comes first, arousing and moving the powers of the soul in the living body. When light strikes the eyes, or sound the ears, the aroused power of the mind calls into action the corresponding species which it holds within, joining them to the outward signs and mixing images with the forms it has hidden in itself.

PROSE 5

To understand this mystery, human reason must contemplate the power of the divine intelligence.

"Thus, in the case of sentient bodies external stimuli affect the sense organs, and a physical sensation precedes the activity of the mind, calling the mind to act upon itself and in

---

[7] Zeno, founder of the Stoic school of philosophers, taught in the Stoa Poekile in Athens. For this reason Boethius calls his followers "philosophers of the Porch."

this way to activate the interior forms which before were inactive. Now if, as I say, in sentient bodies the soul is affected by external bodies but judges these stimuli presented to the body not passively, but by virtue of its own power, how much more do intelligences which are wholly free from all bodily affections use the power of the mind rather than objects extrinsic to themselves in arriving at judgments. According to this principle, various and different substances have different ways of knowing. There are certain immobile living things which are without any means of knowing other than by sense impressions. Shellfish and other forms of marine life which are nourished as they stick to rocks are creatures of this kind. Beasts which have the power of motion, on the other hand, have the impulse to seek and avoid certain things, and they have imagination. But reason is characteristic of the human race alone, just as pure intelligence belongs to God alone.

"It follows, then, that the most excellent knowledge is that which by its own nature knows not only its own proper object but also the objects of all lower kinds of knowledge. What, then, should we think if the senses and imagination were to oppose reason by arguing that the universal, which reason claims to know, is nothing? Suppose they were to argue that whatever can be sensed or imagined cannot be universal; and that therefore either the judgment of reason is true, and there are no objects of sense knowledge, or, since everyone knows that many things can be known by the senses and the imagination, that the conception of reason, which regards whatever is sensible and singular as if it were universal, is vain and empty. And suppose, further, that reason should answer that it conceives sensible and imaginable objects under the aspect of universality, but that the senses and imagination cannot aspire to the knowledge of universality because their knowledge cannot go beyond corporeal figures. Moreover, reason might continue, in matters of knowledge we ought to trust the stronger and more perfect judgment. In such a controversy we who possess the power of reason, as well as of imagination and sense perception, ought to take the side of reason.

"The situation is much the same when human reason supposes that the divine intelligence beholds future events only as reason herself sees them. For you argue that if some things seem not to have certain and necessary outcomes, they cannot be foreknown as certainly about to happen. Therefore, you say that there can be no foreknowledge of these things, or, if we believe that there is such foreknowledge, that the outcome of all things is controlled by necessity. But if we, who are endowed with reason, could possess the intelligence of the divine mind, we would judge that just as the senses and imagination should accede to reason, so human reason ought justly to submit itself to the divine mind. Let us rise, if we can, to the summit of the highest intelligence; for there reason will see what in itself it cannot see: that a certain and definite foreknowledge can behold even those things which have no certain outcome. And this foreknowledge is not mere conjecture but the unrestricted simplicity of supreme knowledge.

POEM 5

"How varied are the shapes of living things on earth! Some there are with bodies stretched out, crawling through the dust, spending their strength in an unbroken furrow; some soar in the air, beating the wind with light wings, floating in easy flight along tracks of air. Some walk along the ground through woods and across green fields. All these, you observe, differ in their varied forms, but their faces look down and cause their senses to grow sluggish.

"The human race alone lifts its head to heaven and stands erect, despising the earth. Man's figure teaches, unless folly has bound you to the earth, that you who look upward with your head held high should also raise your soul to sublime things, lest while your body is raised above the earth, your mind should sink to the ground under its burden.

PROSE 6

Philosophy solves the problem of Providence and free will by distinguishing between simple and conditional necessity.

"Since, as we have shown, whatever is known is known according to the nature of the knower, and not according to its own nature, let us now consider as far as is lawful the nature of the Divine Being, so that we may discover what its knowledge is. The common judgment of all rational creatures holds that God is eternal. Therefore let us consider what eternity is, for this will reveal both the divine nature and divine knowledge.

"Eternity is the whole, perfect, and simultaneous possession of endless life. The meaning of this can be made clearer by comparison with temporal things. For whatever lives in time lives in the present, proceeding from past to future, and nothing is so constituted in time that it can embrace the whole span of its life at once. It has not yet arrived at tomorrow, and it has already lost yesterday; even the life of this day is lived only in each moving, passing moment. Therefore, whatever is subject to the condition of time, even that which—as Aristotle conceived the world to be—has no beginning and will have no end in a life coextensive with the infinity of time, is such that it cannot rightly be thought eternal. For it does not comprehend and include the whole of infinite life all at once, since it does not embrace the future which is yet to come. Therefore, only that which comprehends and possesses the whole plenitude of endless life together, from which no future thing nor any past thing is absent, can justly be called eternal. Moreover, it is necessary that such a being be in full possession of itself, always present to itself, and hold the infinity of moving time present before itself.

"Therefore, they are wrong who, having heard that Plato held that this world did not have a beginning in time and would never come to an end,[8] suppose that the created world

8 *Timaeus* 28ff.

is coeternal with its Creator. For it is one thing to live an endless life, which is what Plato ascribed to the world, and another for the whole of unending life to be embraced all at once as present, which is clearly proper to the divine mind. Nor should God be thought of as older than His creation in extent of time, but rather as prior to it by virtue of the simplicity of His nature. For the infinite motion of temporal things imitates the immediate present of His changeless life and, since it cannot reproduce or equal life, it sinks from immobility to motion and declines from the simplicity of the present into the infinite duration of future and past. And, since it cannot possess the whole fullness of its life at once, it seems to imitate to some extent that which it cannot completely express, and it does this by somehow never ceasing to be. It binds itself to a kind of present in this short and transitory period which, because it has a certain likeness to that abiding, unchanging present, gives everything it touches a semblance of existence. But, since this imitation cannot remain still, it hastens along the infinite road of time, and so it extends by movement the life whose completeness it could not achieve by standing still. Therefore, if we wish to call things by their proper names, we should follow Plato in saying that God indeed is eternal, but the world is perpetual.[9]

"Since, then, every judgment comprehends the subjects presented to it according to its own nature, and since God lives in the eternal present, His knowledge transcends all movement of time and abides in the simplicity of its immediate present. It encompasses the infinite sweep of past and future, and regards all things in its simple comprehension as if they were now taking place. Thus, if you will think about the foreknowledge by which God distinguishes all things, you will rightly consider it to be not a foreknowledge of future events, but knowledge of a never changing present. For this reason, divine knowledge is called providence, rather than prevision, because it resides above all inferior things and looks out on all things from their summit.

9 *Timaeus* 37d ff.

"Why then do you imagine that things are necessary which are illuminated by this divine light, since even men do not impose necessity on the things they see? Does your vision impose any necessity upon things which you see present before you?"

"Not at all," I answered.

"Then," Philosophy went on, "if we may aptly compare God's present vision with man's, He sees all things in his eternal present as you see some things in your temporal present. Therefore, this divine foreknowledge does not change the nature and properties of things; it simply sees things present before it as they will later turn out to be in what we regard as the future. His judgment is not confused; with a single intuition of his mind He knows all things that are to come, whether necessarily or not. Just as, when you happen to see simultaneously a man walking on the street and the sun shining in the sky, even though you see both at once, you can distinguish between them and realize that one action is voluntary, the other necessary; so the divine mind, looking down on all things, does not disturb the nature of the things which are present before it but are future with respect to time. Therefore, when God knows that something will happen in the future, and at the same time knows that it will not happen through necessity, this is not opinion but knowledge based on truth.

"If you should reply that whatever God foresees as happening cannot help but happen, and that whatever must happen is bound by necessity—if you pin me down to this word 'necessity'—I grant that you state a solid truth, but one which only a profound theologian can grasp. I would answer that the same future event is necessary with respect to God's knowledge of it, but free and undetermined if considered in its own nature. For there are two kinds of necessity: one is simple, as the necessity by which all men are mortals; the other is conditional, as is the case when, if you know that someone is walking, he must necessarily be walking. For whatever is known, must be as it is known to be; but this condition does not involve that other, simple necessity. It is not caused by the peculiar nature of the person in question, but by an added condition. No necessity forces the man who is voluntarily walking to move forward; but as long as he is walking, he is necessarily moving forward. In the same way, if Providence sees anything as present, that thing must necessarily be, even though it may have no necessity by its nature. But God sees as present those future things which result from free will. Therefore, from the standpoint of divine knowledge these things are necessary because of the condition of their being known by God; but, considered only in themselves, they lose nothing of the absolute freedom of their own natures.

"There is no doubt, then, that all things will happen which God knows will happen; but some of them happen as a result of free will. And, although they happen, they do not, by their existence, lose their proper natures by which, before they happened, they were able not to happen. But, you may ask, what does it mean to say that these events are not necessary, since by reason of the condition of divine knowledge they happen just as if they were necessary? The meaning is the same as in the example I used a while ago of the sun rising and the man walking. At the time they are happening, they must necessarily be happening; but the sun's rising is governed by necessity even before it happens, while the man's walking is not. Similarly, all the things God sees as present will undoubtedly come to pass; but some will happen by the necessity of their natures, others by the power of those who make them happen. Therefore, we quite properly said that these things are necessary if viewed from the standpoint of divine knowledge, but if they are considered in themselves, they are free of the bonds of necessity. In somewhat the same way, whatever is known by the senses is singular in itself, but universal as far as the reason is concerned.

"But, you may say, if I can change my mind about doing something, I can frustrate Providence, since by chance I may change something which Providence foresaw. My answer is this: you can indeed alter what you propose to do, but, because the present truth of Providence sees that you can, and whether or not you will, you cannot frustrate the divine knowledge any more than you can escape the eye of someone who is present and watching you, even though you may, by your free will, vary your actions. You may still wonder, however, whether God's knowledge is changed by your decisions, so that when you wish now one thing, now another, the divine knowledge undergoes corresponding changes. This is not the case. For divine Providence anticipates every future action and converts it to its own present knowledge. It does not change, as you imagine, foreknowing this or that in succession, but in a single instant, without being changed itself, anticipates and grasps your changes. God has this present comprehension and immediate vision of all things not from the outcome of future events, but from the simplicity of his own nature. In this way, the problem you raised a moment ago is settled. You observed that it would be unworthy of God if our future acts were said to be the cause of divine knowledge. Now you see that this power of divine knowledge, comprehending all things as present before it, itself constitutes the measure of all things and is in no way dependent on things that happen later.

"Since this is true, the freedom of the human will remains inviolate, and laws are just since they provide rewards and punishments to human wills which are not controlled by necessity. God looks down from above, knowing all things, and the eternal present of his vision concurs with the future character of our actions, distributing rewards to the good and punishments to the evil. Our hopes and prayers are not directed to God in vain, for if they are just they cannot fail. Therefore, stand firm against vice and cultivate virtue. Lift up your soul to worthy hopes, and offer humble prayers to heaven. If you will face it, the necessity of virtuous action imposed upon you is very great, since all your actions are done in the sight of a Judge who sees all things."

SUMMARY

Book One. Boethius sets the stage for his dialogue with Philosophy by presenting himself as a man driven almost to despair by adverse fortune. Poetry is his only comfort, or so he thinks, until the vision of a majestic woman appears. She is Philosophy, the personification of the fullest possible achievements of human reason, who stands in figurative opposition to the emotional comforts offered by the Muses of poetry. She offers herself as the only true source of consolation in so extreme a case of human misery.

First, she reminds Boethius of his former strength and intellectual freedom, his former devotion to the wisdom she represents. She reminds him that all her best followers had suffered at the hands of wicked and stupid men, and that it is the duty of the wise and good to oppose them. The wise man stands above good and bad fortune, serene in the strength he derives from self-mastery. But Boethius is too overcome by his misery to understand these general truths; and so, at Philosophy's suggestion, he gives a detailed account of the causes of his despair.

He recalls that he entered the public service because Plato had said that civil government ought to be in the hands of wise men, and that if it were left to the wicked the common good would suffer. He goes on to recount many instances in which his devotion to honesty and justice had embroiled him in conflicts with cruel and venal public officials. In the end, however, he was destroyed by the treachery of corrupt politicians. He was accused of having prevented the enemies of the Senate from giving testimony which would have imputed treason to the Senate, and of having hoped for Roman liberty. Boethius proudly concedes the truth of these charges but denies that he is guilty of any crime. He remarks that he is not surprised at the attack made upon him by wicked men;

but he is appalled that the wicked should overcome the innocent, and he wonders how such injustice can be permitted by God. In spite of his innocence, and his long record of distinguished service, he has been condemned to exile and death by the very body which he sought to protect.

His personal losses are bad enough: he has been ruined professionally, stripped of his possessions, his reputation is destroyed, his liberty lost, and he faces execution. But because his is a wise and public-spirited man, he observes some other more general consequences of his downfall. The attack upon him is an attack upon wisdom and virtue, and the success of his enemies is a victory for the forces of irrationality and evil. Other good men will be terrorized into helplessness by his fate, and evil men will be encouraged in their struggle against public and private virtue.

Philosophy, however, remains unimpressed by this display of self-pity. She says that Boethius' account of his misfortunes reveals an even more desperate weakness in him than she had at first imagined. He has not been driven from his true country of wisdom; he has willfully banished himself from that free city of the self-possessed mind into the land of bondage imposed by false values. She concedes that everything he has said of himself and his unjust treatment is true, but she implies that he is a fool to suppose that justice, in terms of temporal rewards and punishments based on merit, will be found in this life. She observes, however, that for the present he is in no condition to follow her most profound arguments, and so she will lead him gently and slowly to a full understanding of his true condition and the attitude he should take toward it.

She begins by reminding him of the basic truth that the world is governed, not by chance, but by the rational control of the divine Creator. The first book is concluded by Philosophy's general diagnosis of the mental illness suffered by her patient: he has forgotten man's nature and purpose, and so is incapable of understanding the true meaning of what has happened to him. But she can begin with his grasp of the

essential truth of God's government of the world and gradually lead him from the darkness of error to the light of truth.

Book Two. Philosophy begins her treatment with a discourse on the nature of Fortune. It is Fortune's nature to be
changeable, and it is good to know this by personal experience. For no man who has been deceived by Fortune can ever
trust her again; if he puts himself in her power, at least he
will have no illusions about the future. Every man comes into
the world naked, lacking in everything. Whatever temporal
possessions he receives are gifts of that blind and capricious
goddess, given or taken away at the whim of a force whose
only certain characteristic is its mutability.

Boethius acknowledges the general truth of Philosophy's
argument, but he finds it cold comfort for a man in his desperate condition. Philosophy then reminds him of the extraordinary good fortune he has enjoyed up to the time of his
fall; she remarks especially on his adoption by the noble
Symmachus, his happy marriage, his honorable and honored
sons. She also reminds him that the life of man is a temporary
pilgrimage and that death is an end to fortune, whether good
or bad. Again, Boethius admits the truth of Philosophy's argument but observes that the worst part of misfortune is the
memory of the happiness which preceded it. Philosophy remarks sharply that it is silly to suppose that happiness depends on good fortune, and then goes on to remind Boethius
that his most precious possessions, the members of his family,
are still unharmed.

She reminds him that human happiness is neither complete
nor permanent, and that therefore anxiety is a necessary condition of such happiness as men achieve. No one has everything he wants, and no one can be sure of keeping what he
has. True happiness is within, founded on the rational possession of one's self; it cannot be found in the transitory, external gifts of unstable Fortune. For the human soul is immortal, and cannot be satisfied with the kind of happiness
which must end with the death of the body.

Philosophy now begins to examine the various kinds of transitory goods in which men commonly seek happiness. An abundance of material possessions cannot bring happiness, she says, not only because they are easily lost, but because they are external goods which can never fully belong to the one who owns them. Compared to the divine gift of reason, they are lifeless toys which increase our anxiety instead of providing contentment. Nor are public honors and the exercise of power good in themselves. They are more often possessed by the wicked than by the virtuous. None of these gifts of Fortune are good in themselves; whatever goodness is associated with them is to be found in the personal probity of those who may happen to possess them.

Boethius protests that he has not been driven by desire for material possessions and that he has not sought positions of public honor and responsibility for personal satisfaction. Philosophy acknowledges that this is true, but goes on to say that even the fame earned by good men in the performance of important work is a limited and insufficient goal. It is true that excellent men desire glory, but they should remember that such glory is local and short-lived. When the immortal soul is freed from the prison of this world, it will look down from heaven on the earthly fame it sought for and find it an insignificant thing which will ultimately be lost in a kind of second death. Philosophy then concludes the second book by observing that, although the wise man should rise above good and bad Fortune, the latter is actually better—because it is more profitable—than the former. Good fortune tends to enslave the one who enjoys it by deceiving him with specious happiness; bad fortune, however, frees him from the bondage to mutable things by showing him the fragile nature of earthly felicity.

Book Three. Boethius professes to be strengthened by what he has heard so far and to be ready for the stronger medicine of philosophical argument which Philosophy had promised earlier. Philosophy tells him that she will lead him to recognize the nature of true blessedness. It is the nature of man to desire happiness, and perfect happiness can be achieved only in the possession of the supreme good, which contains in itself all lesser goods, and therefore completely and finally fulfills all human desires.

Unfortunately, men are driven by folly and error to mistake limited and transitory objects of desire for this supreme good. They desire riches, or public honors, or power, or fame, or pleasure, or several of these in combination. All these are good, and worthy of desire, and it is natural for men to strive for them; but they are merely partial aspects of the supreme good. Man's troubles arise from treating them as though they were sufficient in themselves. Philosophy then undertakes to show that each of these objects of human desire is insufficient and dangerous. Riches drive men to avarice because they never seem to have enough. Popular acclaim cannot make a man virtuous or wise; indeed, it usually serves to reveal his weaknesses, and besides, such honors are at best temporary. Political power, too, is gravely flawed. The man in power lives in insecurity, full of anxiety and fearful of his enemies and those who profess to be his friends. Fame, too, is a deceptive thing, even for those who merit it by wisdom and virtue; it is limited in time and place, and often rests on unreliable popular judgment. The fame which accompanies noble birth is especially deceptive since it derives from one's ancestors; and, after all, the whole race of men comes from one stock, one father. Thus true nobility is a matter of virtue, and baseness is the product of enslavement to vice. Finally, bodily pleasure cannot lead to perfect happiness. The inordinate satisfaction of bodily appetites caters to the animal part of man's nature and leads only to misery.

Thus all these apparent goods are limited and deceptive; they cannot provide the happiness they seem to promise. True happiness can be found only in the one, all-embracing, perfect good. Human depravity has broken this unity of the good into fragments, and none of the parts can be wholly satisfying. Still, a consideration of false goods can show us the true and perfect happiness which is the full possession of all of them at once. Such happiness can make a man self-sufficient, powerful, worthy of reverence and renown, and full of joy; and the full possession of any one of these necessarily implies the full possession of all the rest.

Philosophy is now approaching the climax of her argument in which she will reveal the only source of this perfect human happiness. In *The Consolation*'s most famous poem, she invokes the inspiration of God, the Creator and Governor of the universe, the perfect Good who is the source of felicity. The poem is followed by her detailed argument in support of the poem's implications. There must be a supreme good, she says, because without some standard of perfection we would not be aware of the relative imperfection and incompleteness of those goods which men habitually pursue. Since God is good, without any imperfection, he must be the supreme good, the source of perfect happiness. But if this is so, it follows that men acquire goodness and happiness by acquiring divinity, by becoming as godlike as their nature allows. The achievement of the supreme good and of perfect happiness are one and the same thing and are found only in God. All other partial and apparent goods are not constituent parts of the supreme good, but aspects of it.

Unity, Philosophy goes on, is the principle of existence. Everything in nature strives to maintain its existence by maintaining its oneness, and to lose this unity of being is to corrupt and die. Since perfect unity is the same as perfect goodness, and since perfect goodness is the same as perfect happiness, all things strive to attain the supreme good as their end or goal. Now, if God, who is the supreme good, is also the ruler of the universe, he must necessarily order and direct all things toward the good. All those, then, who fix their desires on God aspire to true happiness by seeking it at its source. But those who turn their eyes from God and fix their desires on partial, transitory possessions can find only unhappiness. Philosophy illustrates this profound truth with the story of Orpheus told in a poem which concludes the third book.

Book Four. Boethius acknowledges the truth of Philosophy's doctrine that true happiness and the perfect good are the same and are to be found only in God. But how, he asks, can there be evil in a world governed by the omnipotent Good; and, even more puzzling, how is it that this evil not only goes unpunished, but tramples virtue underfoot? Philosophy concedes that it would indeed be monstrous if evil did in fact prevail in the world; but, she says, it does not. Evil men are weak, and never go unpunished; good men are powerful, and virtue is always rewarded. If it is true, she says, that all men seek happiness and desire the good, but only good men can attain these things, it follows that the wicked are powerless to achieve what all men, good and evil, desire. They try to attain the good by unnatural and ineffectual means because they are blinded by ignorance and weakened by intemperance. Worst of all, evil men suffer from lack of existence itself; you can say that they are evil, but you cannot say, in an absolute way, that they *are,* since their very nature is corrupt. Evil is nothing, a negation of true being; hence, the ability to do evil is a weakness, not a power. Furthermore, the good are always rewarded and the evil are always punished. For absolute good is the aim of all human action, but only good men can achieve it. The punishment of the wicked is their wickedness, that loss of goodness which is the loss of human nature. Such men are transformed by vice into beasts.

Boethius acknowledges the truth of Philosophy's argument, but he still regrets that the wicked are permitted to ruin good men. Philosophy, however, argues that this very power is a part of the punishment of the wicked, for their wickedness is the source of their unhappiness. Moreover, they are more unhappy if they remain unpunished than if they are punished, because just punishment is a good which would lessen the evil which is the basis of their misery. If this argument seems incredible to ordinary men, Philosophy observes, that is because ordinary men tend to consult their own feelings rather than the true nature of things. Philosophy further argues that viciousness is a disease of the soul, that the wicked are sick and ought to be regarded with compassion rather than hatred, and that punishment should be regarded as a cure for their sickness.

Boethius, however, is still unable to reconcile himself to a situation in which good men suffer the punishments designed for criminals and wicked men enjoy the rewards intended for the just. In a world governed by chance, these reversals would not be surprising, but in a world ruled by God they seem inexplicable. Philosophy admits that this is the greatest of all philosophical problems, involving the related questions of the relations between Providence and Fate, divine foreknowledge and the freedom of the human will. She will, however, undertake to explain and solve the problem as well as she can. All things that come into being have the cause of their origin, and all the things they do and suffer, in the unchanging mind of God. The government of all mutable natures, insofar as it resides in the divine mind of God, is called Providence; and this same government, looked at with reference to the temporal, mutable things and events which it governs, is called Fate. Providence is the divine reason itself by which all things are ordered; Fate is that order and disposition as it is seen in the unfolding of events in time. Thus, the operations of Fate may seem confused and discordant, but that is because human judgment is often incapable of discerning the providential order by which they are governed. God's providence is wise and good, whether or not we are able to comprehend it. All fortune is good, since it has as its purpose the reward or testing of good men, or the correction and punishment of the wicked.

Book Five. Boethius now wonders whether Philosophy's doctrine of God's providential government of all things leaves any room for chance. Philosophy replies that if by chance we mean an event without causes, then there can be no such thing. But if we mean simply an event whose causes are neither foreseen nor expected, then chance does exist.

At this point Boethius raises the inevitable and profound question of the possibility of free human choice in a world governed by divine Providence. Philosophy replies that every rational nature must have free will, for the power of judgment and decision necessarily implies the power to choose between what should be desired and what should be shunned. But, she continues, the exercise of this power depends on clarity of judgment and integrity of will, so that men who are blinded and corrupted by enslavement to their passions cannot see clearly and choose freely. Now Boethius raises the most difficult problem of all. If God, with the perfect clarity of divine vision foresees everything, and if whatever his providence foresees must happen, how can man be free to choose what he desires? If the outcome of human events can depend on the free choices of men, they must be uncertain and unnecessary, and, if so, how can God know them? On the other hand, if nothing can be uncertain to Him who is the certain cause of all things, whatever He knows will happen, must happen. Boethius sees the implications of his argument. If men cannot choose freely, then the entire social structure of rewards for the good and punishment for the wicked breaks down; vice and virtue are without meaning, and God himself must be held responsible for the evil which He determines. Prayer would be meaningless, since everything is determined by God's unalterable foreknowledge. All this is unthinkable, but Boethius sees no way out of the dilemma.

Philosophy answers that the cause of confusion in this important matter lies in the fact that human reason is incapable of comprehending the simplicity and perfection of divine knowledge. Men assume that God must know in the way that human reason knows, and so they ascribe to God's knowledge the limitations they find in their own. Human reason properly regards future events as uncertain, if their outcomes are unknown, or as necessary, if their outcomes are known with certainty. But the divine intelligence, unlimited by dependence on time, sees all things not as past, present, and future, but as eternally present. For eternity is the whole, perfect, and simultaneous possession of endless life. Thus, God does not, properly speaking, have foreknowledge but knowledge of a never changing present; He sees things as present as they will later turn out to be in what we regard as the future. And in this way He sees things which happen through free human choice as well as things which happen through necessity.

It is true, Philosophy goes on, that what God sees as happening must necessarily happen; but in the case of things freely chosen by men the necessity is found only in God's knowledge of the event, not in the nature of the event itself. All things will happen which God knows will happen, but some of them will happen as a result of man's free will. Nor is God's knowledge changed by our changes of mind. Providence anticipates every future action and sees immediately what seems to us a succession of choices and actions. The freedom of the human will is inviolate and imposes upon men a grave obligation to act virtuously, for all their actions are done in the sight of a Judge who sees all things and rewards and punishes according to his perfect knowledge.

INDEX